Effective Practice in the EYFS

An Essential Guide

Effective Practice in the EYFS

An Essential Guide

Vicky Hutchin

 Open University Press

Open University Press
McGraw-Hill Education
McGraw-Hill House
Shoppenhangers Road
Maidenhead
Berkshire
England
SL6 2QL

email: enquiries@openup.co.uk
world wide web: www.openup.co.uk

and Two Penn Plaza, New York, NY 10121-2289, USA

First published 2013

A catalogue record of this book is available from the British Library

ISBN-13: 978-0-33-524753-0
ISBN-10: 0335247539
e-ISBN: 978-0-33-524754-7
Library of Congress Cataloging-in-Publication Data

CIP data applied for
Typeset by Aptara, Inc.

Printed and bound by CPI Group (UK) Ltd, Croydon, CR0 4YY
Fictitious names of companies, products, people, characters and/or data
that may be used herein (in case studies or in examples) are not intended
to represent any real individual, company, product or event.

Praise for this book

"*Effective Practice in the EYFS* is a clear, comprehensive and accessible exposition of the new EYFS and its requirements for practitioners. Using case studies, examples from settings and observations of children, Vicky Hutchin brings breadth and depth to each aspect of the EYFS and ensures that practitioners have a principled understanding of the importance and relevance of each aspect of their work with young children. The Characteristics of Early Learning are given appropriate significance and can be seen to underpin all subsequent chapters. The Prime and Specific Areas of Learning are each highlighted with great clarity and every chapter concludes with 'Top Tips for Effective Practice' which could be used to create a development plan by any setting wanting to reflect on current practice. This book would be valuable for all practitioners but particularly those new to the early years and wanting a clear reference guide to all that is important about teaching in this phase.

Julie Fisher, Independent Early Years Advisor

"This book will guide practitioners on their journey into the new requirements of the EYFS, and will build confidence. It is written with clarity, encourages common sense and draws on the good practice of real settings together with useful reference to research and literature. Just what is needed!"

Professor Tina Bruce CBE, University of Roehampton, UK

"As an Essential Guide to the revised EYFS Vicky Hutchin's book covers *everything* a practitioner needs to know and think about. The emphasis on the Characteristics of Effective Learning ensures that the reader understands right from the outset that HOW children learn rather than WHAT they learn is a priority. There are clear explanations of the Characteristics which are underpinned by the theory of how children learn and develop, including important connections to the psychology of children's early learning.

Vicky has woven together the statutory requirements of the EYFS with examples of good early years practice and the voice of the child. The central strand of observation and interpreting how children are learning supports practitioners' understanding and gives them helpful directions to the work of Ferre Laevers, Julie Fisher and others.

There is a strong reflective element running through the book with helpful case studies, questions to think about and useful summaries at the end of each chapter. Chapter 12 helpfully directs the reader to think about the EYFS as an evaluative tool to improve the quality of practice.

These are the strengths of Vicky's book along with the following
- A good explanation of school readiness
- Clear explanations of child initiated and adult- led thinking and learning
- Links to parental involvement throughout the book as well as a dedicated chapter
- Assessment which is child focussed and based in the context of observation and planning next steps. The messages are clear and respectful of children
- Unpicking each area of learning and making the links between theory and practice as well as a frequent reminder of the holistic nature of children's development and learning
- Top tips for effective practice and points for reflection"

Di Chilvers, Advisory Consultant in Early Childhood

Contents

Acknowledgements

A special thanks goes to the settings and schools, practitioners and parents who have generously contributed their observations of children, written summative assessments and numerous opportunities to discuss their work with me. I would also like to thank the children for their own mark making and the photographs. In particular I would like to thank the following settings and practitioners: Michael Pettavel, Lizzie Hutt and the staff team especially the Under Threes team, at Randolph Beresford Early Years Centre, London; Jackie Feeney and especially Myrtle Nixon at Old Oak Community & Children's Centre, London; Peter Catling and the Under Threes staff team at Woodlands Park Nursery School and Children's Centre, London; Marcelo Staricoff and Robb Johnson at Hertford Infants School, Brighton and Wendy Plater and the staff team at Bright Start Nursery, Brighton for photographs.

This book could not have been written without the unconditional support of Billy Ridgers, who took photographs, and read and commented on copious drafts. Thank you Billy.

All photographs, including the cover photograph, are by Billy Ridgers, 2012.

Introduction: The Revised EYFS 2012 and Effective Practice

Please note: throughout the book the term 'parents' is used to refer to the child's main carers, who is usually, but not always, the child's parents.

Everyone in England who works with children from birth to 5 in a school, early years setting or as a childminder does so within the framework of the revised Early Years Foundation Stage (EYFS) 2012. This Statutory Framework, known as the Statutory Framework for the Early Years Foundation Stage, spells out the legal requirements and regulations, covering what providers and practitioners need to do to ensure children are safe, healthy and well looked after, and to support their learning and development. It is divided into three sections: the learning and development requirements, assessment requirements, and safeguarding and welfare requirements.

This book explores the learning and development, and assessment aspects of the EYFS 2012 with a clear focus on effective practice. Each chapter makes links between the EYFS and the theory and research that underpins it. We have a long tradition of excellent early years practice in Britain, backed up by well-evidenced research. Throughout the book there are examples of effective practice in action, taken from a number of such settings, where the staff constantly reflect on their practice to ensure the best provision for the children. There are also observations of children learning and developing as they play and explore the world around them and challenge themselves, as well as quotations from practitioners about aspects of their work.

Key features of the revised EYFS

When the EYFS was first introduced in 2008 it was welcomed by many practitioners because of its principled approach and comprehensive coverage of young children's learning and development as well as the breadth of official, government endorsed guidance materials on how to support this. The revised EYFS has few such 'non-statutory' guidance materials, one of the few being the main guidance document 'Development Matters in the Early Years Foundation Stage' (Early Education, 2012). You will find the 'official' guidance materials listed in the references at the end of this book.

The revisions to the EYFS in 2012 made some significant changes, but most of these build on the strong foundations laid in the first version in 2008. The rationale behind the changes can be found in the initial review document to the EYFS, 'The Early Years: Foundations for Life, Health and Learning' (Tickell, 2011), generally known as the 'Tickell Review'. This is a thought-provoking and detailed document, which set the EYFS on course for the current Statutory Framework 2012. Because of this it is frequently referred to in this book.

The principles

The revised EYFS 2012 is based on a set of four themes and principles (see Table I.1).

The guidance document, Development Matters (2012), shows how these four themes work together to support children, setting it out in a formula:

A unique child + positive relationships + enabling environments = learning and development (Early Education, 2012)

How children learn

The revised EYFS emphasises how children learn, by taking three important aspects of the original 2008 EYFS – 'Play and

Table I.1   The EYFS principles

A Unique Child	Positive Relationships	Enabling Environments	Learning and Development
Every child is a unique child who is constantly learning and can be resilient, capable, confident and self-assured	Children learn to be strong and independent through positive relationships	Children learn and develop well in enabling environments in which their experiences respond to their individual needs and there is a strong partnership between practitioners, parents and carers	The framework covers the education and care of all children in early years provision, including children with special educational needs and disabilities

Exploration', 'Active Learning' and 'Creativity and Critical Thinking' – and making them more prominent than ever before. Understanding how children learn is essential if we are to support their learning effectively. These are now called the 'Characteristics of Effective Learning' and become the starting point for this book, the topic for Chapter 1.

In Chapter 2, points made in Chapter 1 about how children learn are followed up by considering the role of practitioner in supporting learning effectively. After that, we look, in Chapter 3, at an area that is taking on increasing importance in recent years: developing a strong, positive partnership with parents.

The areas of learning and development

There are seven areas of learning and development in the revised EYFS, replacing the six areas in the previous (2008) EYFS. These are organised into two sets: the prime and the specific areas. Chapters 4 to 10 each consider a different area of learning and development, starting with the three prime areas, as described on the next page.

The prime areas

The revised EYFS has taken a new look at the areas of learning and development, acknowledging that Personal, Social and Emotional Development, Communication and Language, and Physical Development are much more fundamentally linked to child development than the other areas. 'These play a crucial role... in laying the cornerstones for healthy development. Without secure development in these particular areas during this critical period, children will struggle to progress' (Tickell, 2011: 20). They are universal in every child's development, regardless of social or cultural context. The three areas are closely interconnected.

The specific areas

The four specific areas of learning and development are Literacy, Mathematics, Understanding the World, and Expressive Arts and Design. The specific areas tend to relate more to bodies of knowledge and sets of skills that we want children to learn, such as literacy and mathematics. As the Tickell Review states: 'These specific areas of learning are influenced by the times we live in and our beliefs about what it is important for children to learn' (Tickell, 2011: 96).

The specific areas are dependent on the prime areas: young children learn about them through relationships with others, communicating with others and physical action. But the prime are not dependent on the specific. It is not a question of first the prime and then the specific, as learning in the specific areas begins as we introduce babies and toddlers to a wide range of experiences, such as the world of books and things to explore. It is important to be aware that young children do not see the separation between the areas of learning and development. They should not be presented as 'subjects' to be learned, but as a part of everyday, enjoyable experiences of positive, supportive relationships, play and playful interactions with others in an enabling environment.

Observing and assessing learning and development

A key skill for practitioners working with young children is the ability to observe the children and analyse what has been observed in order to make an assessment. We cannot plan effectively for children's learning and development without observing them. This is ongoing formative assessment, a crucial aspect of effective practice.

In addition to this, there are now two statutory summative assessments to be made by practitioners in the EYFS: the Progress Check at Age Two and the EYFS Profile at the end of a child's time in the EYFS phase, when most children are in reception classes. Chapter 11 considers both formative and summative assessment, with a particular focus on the Progress Check at Age Two.

The Safeguarding and Welfare Requirements

The third section of the EYFS Statutory Framework is the Safeguarding and Welfare Requirements. This sets out the minimum standards for ensuring children's welfare, health, wellbeing and safety; these cover aspects of provision such as child protection, suitable people (to work with the children), qualifications and training, the 'key person' role, staff–child ratios, food and drink, accidents, safety and suitability of premises, equipment and the environment. The key person role, so vital for children's wellbeing and successful learning, is discussed in detail in Chapter 2.

School readiness?

One of the first points you will notice in the introduction to the revised Statutory Framework is that the EYFS is about 'school readiness': 'It promotes teaching and learning to ensure children's "school readiness"' (EYFS, 2012: 11). However, this term is never defined and consequently there has been much deliberation in England about what it really means. Effective provision for children's learning and development is so much more than getting them ready to attend school! Most of us working in the early years would prefer to think about enabling the children in our care to be happy and confident children during their time in the setting, developing the resilience to deal with the challenges of future life, and to become curious, inquisitive and interested individuals with a love of learning.

'School readiness' is widely debated in the United States too, and has been for some time. In their research paper, 'Readiness for School: A Survey of State Policies and Definitions', Saluja *et al.* (2000) reviewed state policies in the United States with regards to school readiness. They found little consistency in definition or policy between one state and another. However, they make an important point about the need for schools to be ready for all children. The authors quote the 'Ten Keys to Ready Schools' by Shore (1998):

> Ready schools should have strong leadership, strive for continuity between early care and education programmes, promote smooth transitions between home and school, be committed to the success of every child as well as every teacher and adult who interacts with children at school, use approaches that have been shown to raise children's achievement and then alter practices and programmes if they do not benefit children. (quoted in Saluja *et al.*, 2000)

In England, at around the time of the publication of the Tickell Review, two other government-commissioned reviews relating to early years were published: 'Families in the Foundation Years', by Frank Field (2010), and the Graham Allen Review (2011): 'Early Intervention: The Next Step'. Both of these discuss 'school readiness' at some length and, whereas the Graham Allen Review refers to this as being linked to children's 'social and emotional wellbeing' (Allen, 2011: 54), Frank Field defines it as being about the child's communication and language development, social and emotional development and physical development. Finally, the

Tickell Review considers what it might mean for a child to be 'unready' for school:

> My view is that the skills a child needs for school are part of the skills they need for life. We all want our children to lead happy, enquiring, active childhoods, recognising that this provides the foundations for fulfilled and productive adulthoods.

She goes on to say:

> The evidence is clear that children who are behind in their development at age 5 are much more likely than their peers to be behind still at age 7, and this can lead to sustained but avoidable underachievement. (Tickell, 2011: 19)

Reflecting on practice

The main aims of this book are to help readers understand the revised EYFS, effectively implement it and reflect on what they are already doing to support children's learning, development and wellbeing, and to think about what else can be done to make it even better. For this reason, the section in each chapter (except Chapter 2) entitled 'Top Tips for Effective Practice' summarises key points, followed by a point for reflection for readers to mull over with colleagues or on their own. Chapter 2 summarises each section in a slightly different way and has two points for reflection.

As you read each chapter, find a child or group of children to observe in different contexts, illustrating for yourself what learning and development might look like in the various aspects of the EYFS. Not only will this provide you with your own personally observed example, but it is also one of the best ways of learning about how children develop, learn, think and act.

1 The Characteristics of Effective Learning

At the very beginning of the review that led to the revised EYFS in 2012 the author, Dame Clare Tickell, tells us: 'A child's future choices, attainment, wellbeing, happiness and resilience are profoundly affected by the quality of guidance, love and care they receive during their first years' (Tickell, 2011: 2). To provide this quality we need to start by understanding as much as we can about how children learn and develop. In fact, in the EYFS 2012, this has even been made a statutory requirement!

> *In planning and guiding children's activities practitioners must reflect on the different ways that children learn and reflect these in their practice.* (EYFS, 2012: 1.10)

The EYFS has always highlighted the importance of *how* as well as *what* children learn. In the 2008 EYFS this was most obvious in three of the commitments under the theme of Learning and Development: *Play and Exploration, Active Learning* and *Creativity and Critical Thinking*. The Tickell Review in 2011 pledged to strengthen the importance of how children learn as fundamental to effective practice, renaming these three commitments as the 'Characteristics of Effective Learning' and giving them greater prominence by devoting a section of the report to them. Although there is little information on them in the revised Statutory Framework, it has been made a requirement for reception teachers to provide information to Year 1 teachers on how each child has been learning in relation to the 'Characteristics', as part of the statutory assessment the EYFS Profile.

Table 1.1 The Characteristics of Effective Learning

Playing and exploring
- *finding out and exploring*
- *playing with what they know*
- *being willing to have a go*

Active learning
- *being involved and concentrating*
- *keeping on trying*
- *enjoying achieving what they set out to do*

Creating and thinking critically
- *having their own ideas*
- *making links*
- *choosing ways to do things and finding new ways*

In the non-statutory guidance, 'Development Matters', each characteristic is divided into three elements to clarify what it involves. With the help of some observations of children learning, playing, doing and thinking, some of the theory underpinning each characteristic will be explained.

Playing and exploring

Play and exploration are key ways that children (and adults) learn. As Vygotsky, the famous Russian psychologist whose work has been so important to our understanding of child development, stated: in play the child operates at their highest level 'beyond his average age, above his daily behaviour; in play it is as though he were a head taller than himself' (Vygotsky, 1978: 102). This is why it is so powerful. Because it is so important to learning, the revised Statutory Framework states that:

> *Each area of learning and development must be implemented through planned and purposeful play and a mix of adult led and child initiated activity.* (EYFS, 2012: 1.9)

Finding out and exploring

Exploratory play is important to all of us. It is how babies begin to understand their surroundings and the relationships between themselves and others, using all their senses and every part of the body. Gopnik *et al.* (1999) describe babies and toddlers as young scientists, testing out and often repeating the same actions time and again to establish an idea about the object in question and what their own actions can do. Their explorations continue as they grow and develop.

Khyra is 2 yrs 6 mths. Today there is a large tray out on the table, and a bag of flour is being tipped out on to it. Khyra dips her hands in, then spreads the flour with her hands making swirling movements, deeply involved in watching the patterns she makes for a short while, then clapping her hands together, laughing as she does so. A few days later, the flour is put out again, but this time with water in a jug. She tips the water into the flour and feels it with her fingers, then her hands, squishing and squashing the sticky mixture as she explores the texture. Again, she is deeply involved and we can almost see the questions in her head: What is this? What does it do and what can I do with it? Such simple provision provides opportunities to explore and play with an experience rich in learning opportunities.

Playing with what they know

From the beginning as they play and explore, babies and young children build a repertoire of knowledge, skills and understanding, using memory, and they are also able to imagine possibilities. This makes it possible for them to play with what they know.

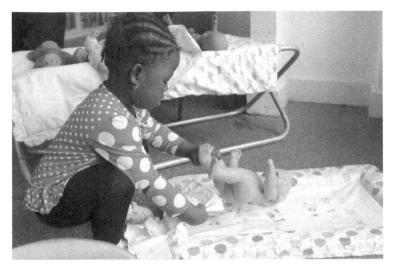

Figure 1.1

Kimarla, also aged 2 yrs 6 mths, is using her knowledge of nappy changing and care of babies, and the care she has received, as she first pretends to change this doll's nappy (Fig 1.1) then later returns to the home corner, dressed up (Fig 1.2), to pretend to feed herself. No one has suggested either of these activities, it is her own choice, but the practitioners have provided the environment and resources they know she and others will want to make use of.

Being willing to 'have a go'

Play is the ideal context for trying things out, taking risks, making mistakes and challenging ourselves – in other words, being willing to have a go. As Vivian Gussin Paley, whose work has taught us so much about child development and play, says: 'There is no activity children are better prepared for than fantasy play. Nothing is more dependable and risk-free, and the dangers are only pretend' (Paley, 2004: 8).

Figure 1.2

Play builds children's confidence, because, in play, the child is in control. The subject matter, the nature of the play and the direction it takes must be the decision of the child or children, if it is play. In play, the children choose the theme, when to start and when to stop, and what will be involved. They can decide to move in and out of play at any point or repeat it as much as they like. Play helps us come to terms with fears, dangers, and the unpredictability of the world and human relationships. As adults, we can support and facilitate play, but if we take control of it, it is no longer the child's agenda and is unlikely to bring about learning. The adult role in play is discussed further in Chapter 2.

Louis, aged just 3 years, is playing in his nursery setting with small-world animals. He has tipped them all out of the box and now begins to line some up in twos, nose to tail. He holds up two face to face, a lion and a lion cub, and we can hear him talking for them: 'You go first baby!' 'No, I'm scared.' 'Quick, quick the monster's coming! Hide!' He hides them under the upturned box.

In his play we see him creating his own story, in which a great deal of knowledge and understanding is being used. The play is helping him to:

- explore what it might feel like to be someone or something else
- be in control
- explore relationships and negotiation skills
- manage feelings that may be frightening or enjoyable
- devise problems and be the one who solves them
- develop communication skills
- apply existing skills and knowledge in new ways, as well as those that are in the process of being learned and developed.

Active learning

The second characteristic of learning is not about being physically active, which of course is important in children's learning and development, but refers to being *mentally* active and alert.

As we see in Table 1.1, it involves children in becoming deeply involved and concentrating, being motivated to persist (keep on trying) and deriving satisfaction from achieving what they have chosen to do. Those close to the child – parents and practitioners – can foster this inner drive to learn and achieve, supporting a can-do approach and building confidence, or we can all too easily discourage it.

In the Tickell Review active learning was described as arising from the 'intrinsic motivation to achieve mastery – to experience competence, understanding and autonomy' (Tickell, 2011: 90).

Being involved and concentrating

In order to concentrate fully on something we need to be motivated. Concentration is closely linked to the concept of involvement. The research of Ferre Laevers has shown that when children are deeply involved in what they are doing, it is likely that *deep-level learning* is taking place. And, 'if deep-level learning is taking place, a person is operating at the limits of their "zone of proximal development"' (Laevers, 2000). When a child is deeply involved she/he cannot easily be distracted. The importance of play and exploration cannot be underestimated as it is when children make their own choices, follow their natural curiosity and own train of thought that deep involvement is most likely to happen. All three children discussed earlier – Khyra, Kimarla and Louis – were deeply involved and concentrating in their play.

Keeping on trying

Keeping on trying, as it is called, is all about persistence, being motivated to master a new skill or understand a new idea, even though this may require considerable effort. The research of Carol Dweck over the past few decades has been significant in helping us understand why some children and adults are more prone to persisting when faced with a challenge than others and what we can do to help this. Dweck has identified that how we see ourselves as learners is the root of the issue, whether we have a 'fixed mindset', with a self-belief that tells us that our abilities are fixed and cannot be changed, or a 'growth mindset', through which we believe our abilities can grow and develop.

For those with a fixed mindset there is a desire to get things right from the start so as not to feel a failure, wanting to stay in the safety zone of what they know they can achieve, not taking on any new challenge: 'As soon as children become able to evaluate themselves, some of them are afraid of challenges. They become afraid of not being smart' (Dweck, 2008: 16). The opposite is true for those with the growth mindset, who love a challenge and will therefore keep on trying, find a way around obstacles and figure out the problem.

Figure 1.3 Persisting and mastering a new skill

Dweck believes that adults can all too easily limit children's motivation and drive to take on new challenges. How we give children praise is really important, praising a child for 'being clever' and for their abilities is more likely to result in developing the fixed mindset view of themselves, not wanting to persist when difficulties appear. But specific praise highlighting the processes the child is using as they attempt to do something, or keep on trying, will feed the growth mindset.

> When we receive encouragement for our efforts and our ideas are valued, our feelings acknowledged and our discoveries recognised, we come to see the world as a safe place, and ourselves as competent and capable agents within it. (National Strategies, 2007: 3)

Enjoying achieving what they set out to do

Following on from persistence is the satisfaction gained from achieving *one's own* intentions 'rather than relying on the approval of others' (Tickell, 2011: 90). The emphasis here is on the children achieving *their own* goals, whatever these might be: to be successful and enjoy the personal pleasure of success, the goal needs to be the child's. This will mean the child is fully signed up to it and the motivation is intrinsic, coming from within. If the motivation is extrinsic, arising from a perceived external reward, then once the reward has been achieved there is little motivation to continue. We need to take care presenting children with rewards. This is important when it comes to goals we want children to achieve. Tapping into the child's curiosity and interests is likely to help them make the goal their own, resulting in better longer-term outcomes.

Creating and thinking critically

The guidance materials for the 2008 EYFS provided a useful description of this learning characteristic:

> When children have opportunities to play with ideas in different situations and with a variety of resources, they discover connections and come to new and better understandings and ways of doing things. Adult support in this process enhances their ability to think critically and ask questions. (EYFS card 4.3, 2008)

Creating and thinking critically are fundamental processes in making sense of experiences and developing thought. Creativity in this sense is not about being talented in the arts, but a core aspect of the thinking process, involving imagination and helping us 'to think flexibly … and come up with original ideas' (Stewart, 2011: 78). Thinking critically helps us to organise our thoughts, figure things out, solve problems and come up with new strategies. It helps us reflect on ideas and on our own thinking, and from this learn how to learn.

Having their own ideas

In order to be able to solve problems in their daily experiences, children, like adults, need to generate their own ideas and put these to good use. Play and exploration are fundamental to this, something we as parents or practitioners close to the child should be encouraging children to do so that they can develop their own ideas: 'Being inventive allows children to find new problems as they seek challenge and to explore ways of solving these' (Tickell, 2011: 90).

Enabling children to think critically and creatively means encouraging them to play and investigate, providing a rich environment with interesting things to discover, explore and wonder about and, crucially, time to do so. Some of the most important skills children need for the future are the metacognitive skills, which involve them in reflecting on their learning: 'Awareness of oneself as a thinker and learner is a key aspect of success in learning' (Tickell, 2011: 90).

Making links

As babies and young children make sense of their experiences, they are making connections between what they already know and new experiences. We can see the baby or toddler making these connections through their play and explorations, and later as children begin to communicate verbally, they are able to express their thoughts and ideas to themselves (as in the observation of Louis, above), as well as to others.

Communication is an important aspect of the thinking process and the more open-ended the discussions we have with young children the more we can help them talk about the connections they are making and as a result understand their own thinking better. Recent research quoted in the Early Years Learning and Development Review in 2009 showed that when children are asked to say how they solved a problem they learned more than when they were just given positive feedback on solving the problem (Evangelou *et al.,* 2009).

Choosing ways to do things

This aspect of the Characteristics of Learning involves the child in making choices as to how to go about something and is not about following instructions. It involves 'making choices and decisions about how to approach a task, planning and monitoring what to do, and being able to change strategies' (Tickell, 2011: 91). It is when children are involved in their own self-chosen activities that they are more likely to want to find the right strategy to achieve their goal.

Top tips for effective practice

The Characteristics of Effective Learning are generic: they are about how every child learns. But, to support children's learning and development effectively, we need to pay attention to the uniqueness of every child. In this section we look very briefly at how settings and practitioners can best support children's learning and development by paying attention to these Characteristics of Effective Learning. The next chapter spells out in more detail specific elements of the role of the practitioner.

- **Talking with parents:** supporting children's learning and development starts with finding out about them from those who know them best, their parents, and working in close partnership with them.
- **Ensuring inclusion** means being aware of the different ways that children learn and ensuring that planning supports each unique child.
- **Tuning in and following children's interests** is essential if practitioners are to meet the learning and development needs of every child. This means observing and listening first, so that you can tailor your input to what the child is focusing on.
- **Building confidence and a can-do attitude:** being positive, providing emotional support, encouraging children to have a go.
- **Encouraging the children to make their own choices** as well as decisions on how they may want to do things.

- **Taking care with how you praise** is important in helping children to develop a *growth mindset*. Talk with them about the strategies they are using as they attempt new challenges and solve problems. Give praise for trying, not for 'being clever'.
- **Providing a stimulating environment,** inside and outside, not only responds to children's interests, but also provokes new ones.
- **Motivate and challenge children's thinking,** with opportunities for them to explore, investigate and solve problems, and plenty to fire the imagination, with and without adult support. A child who is not given the opportunity to play, explore and investigate is far less likely to be a resilient, creative learner willing to have a go, persist or think critically.
- **Allow time for children to think and reflect.**
- **Remember that play and exploration** are fundamental to learning and thinking.

Point for reflection

It is worth having a look at the wealth of guidance and resources provided in the EYFS 2008, which include research papers about children's learning and effective practice information, remembering that the major change in 2012 was changes to the areas of learning and development and the statutory assessments. The 'Commitment Cards' and other guidance resources remain as useful as ever. These are available on the EYFS CD-ROM. If you cannot find the EYFS CD-ROM, go to https://www.education.gov.uk/publications/ standard/publicationDetail/Page1/DCSF-00261-2008.

2 Supporting Young Children's Learning and Development

Children do not learn in isolation and the role of adults is central: it can enable children to become capable, confident, creative and resilient learners, or it can limit possibilities. The purpose of this chapter is to unpick the complexities of an effective adult role in supporting children's learning and development in the EYFS, before we make the journey around the areas of learning and development. We begin by looking at an important statutory requirement, the 'key person' role. We then move on to consider how to support children's learning effectively through play and activities, moment by moment.

The 'key person' role

The key person is one of the most important requirements of the EYFS for the practitioner. In a setting it requires a member of staff to be allocated to a small number of children (a key group) to whom they become the key person; for a childminder this means all children in his/her care. This is a role with a very special responsibility, designed to provide continuity between home and setting, and ensure that a close supportive relationship is maintained between the child with one individual in the setting: 'The key person makes sure that, within the day-to-day demands of a setting each child feels individual, cherished and thought about by someone in particular while they are away from home' (Elfer *et al.*, 2002: 18).

The key person role, a requirement in the EYFS since 2008, has been further strengthened in the revised 2012 EYFS:

Each child must be assigned a key person (a safeguarding and welfare requirement). Providers must inform parents and/or carers of the name of the key person, and explain their role, when a child starts attending a setting. The key person must help ensure that every child's learning and care is tailored to meet their individual needs. The key person must seek to engage and support parents and/or carers in guiding their child's development at home. (EYFS, 2012: 1.11)

It is the final sentence that has strengthened the key person role and depends on a 'triangle of trust and communication' (Goldschmied and Selleck, 1996) between key person, parents and child to be successful. We look at this in more detail in Chapter 3.

Attachment

The rationale for the key person role stems from the concept of attachment, the baby and young child's basic need for a close emotional bond to another person, usually the mother, who will provide the necessary sense of belonging, nurture, care and responsiveness. It is through this attachment that babies and young children gain the security, confidence and resilience to become independent. It helps the child form positive relationships and provides the emotional security necessary for cognitive development to flourish.

What are the expectations?

There are high expectations of the key person: a professional role, requiring considerable skill. Responsibilities include being the person who:

- builds the closest relationship with the child and the family in the setting
- gets to know the child well and responds to their needs
- parents leave the child with every day
- provides consistency in care and attention

- makes links with parents on a day-to-day basis and regularly makes time to talk with parents about their child
- parents talk to if they have concerns about their child.

Lizzie, under threes team leader in a Children's Centre, described the role in this way:

A huge part of our ethos is being an advocate for the child, and in particular we see this as the key person's role. As well as getting to know the child best of all and building the closest relationships with the family, the key person helps to ensure that their key children get their entitlement to a supportive enriching environment which supports their learning and development. They may also be an advocate for the child if professionals from different agencies are involved in supporting the child and family.

Organising the key person role

Being a key person can sound like a daunting task, but with careful management and a whole-setting approach it is the most rewarding and fulfilling role in the early years. With it comes job satisfaction and a sense of self-worth – you matter to the child and family. It brings with it the joy of a close, caring relationship, playing a part in their child's learning and development.

Effective teamwork

It requires effective teamwork and consistency of approach throughout the setting – for example, making sure every team member is aware of the responsibilities and how to carry these out. Making time for staff to discuss their key children at planning and daily evaluation meetings will help to establish this.

In daycare settings or settings with many part-time staff, it is important to consider how to provide the consistent relationship for the child and family when the key person is not there. It is most common to organise staff teams into pairs, as in Lizzie's setting:

> *Each child has a key person and a co-key person too, as the staff are on shifts. The co-key person takes charge of the child if their key person is not present. Every family knows who their child's co-key person is.*

Supervision

To support the development of the role, the revised Statutory Framework has made 'supervision' of staff a requirement – a time where staff can have a professional discussion about their work with the children.

> *Supervision should provide opportunities for staff to:*
> - *discuss any issues – particularly concerning children's development or wellbeing;*
> - *identify solutions to address issues as they arise; and*
> - *receive coaching to improve their personal effectiveness.*
> (Statutory Framework, 2012: 3.20)

Tried and tested strategies

The key person role is statutory for all types of setting, regardless of staff–child ratios. The following are examples of strategies that effective settings use to ensure the best for every child.

- Each child is welcomed by their key person when they arrive and the key person is available to talk with parents. This means group times do not take place at the beginning of the session.
- The key person is responsible for intimate care such as nappy changing and toileting.
- Meals are taken in key person groups.
- Group sessions such as story/song time are with the key person. However, this works best when the key group is children of similar ages and stages of development.

- The key person is in charge of *collating* and summarising records (observations, photos, etc.), but in a group setting they will not be the only person writing the observations.

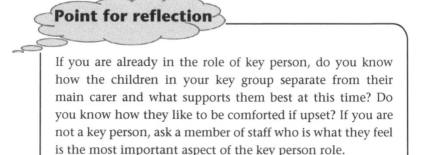

Point for reflection

If you are already in the role of key person, do you know how the children in your key group separate from their main carer and what supports them best at this time? Do you know how they like to be comforted if upset? If you are not a key person, ask a member of staff who is what they feel is the most important aspect of the key person role.

The adult role in supporting learning

Observing: a core part of the adult role

Fundamental to supporting children's learning and development effectively is 'tuning in' to them through observing. As one nursery teacher said: 'It's about seeing something happen with a child. You need to think about what is happening then suddenly you start to understand what is going on and you begin to work out how you can intervene appropriately to support the child' (Hutchin, 2010: 38).

Observing is a core part of the practitioner role as it is from this that we make decisions about how best to support the children. As you read the next section you will see frequent references to the need to observe, or watch and listen to gauge what the child is doing and showing interest in. We cannot ignore children's interests, as this is what motivates them most.

Effective support

Effective support for learning is subtle and complex, and only a small part of it is about direct instruction. The revised Statutory

Framework, as we saw in Chapter 1, makes implementing a 'mix of adult-led and child-initiated activity' a requirement. So what do we mean by 'child-initiated and adult-led activity', and how do we support play? One of the 'official' EYFS guidance documents for the original 2008 EYFS explained the effective adult role in supporting learning more fully:

> The best outcomes for children's learning occur when most of the activity within a child's day is a mixture of child initiated play, actively supported by adults and focused learning, with adults guiding the learning through playful, rich experiential activities. Too little adult support can limit learning ... too much tightly directed activity deprives children of the opportunity to engage actively with learning. (National Strategies, 2009b: 5)

Findings from research

The findings of Researching Effective Pedagogy in the Early Years (REPEY) (Siraj-Blatchford *et al.*, 2002), part of the longitudinal Effective Provision of Preschool Education (EPPE) project (1997 and ongoing), have been significant in developing our understanding of effective support for young children's learning. The REPEY research looked in detail at the settings in EPPE where outcomes for children were highest. A major finding was that: 'In the excellent and good settings the balance of who initiated the activities, child or adult, was very equal, revealing that the pedagogy of these effective settings encourages children to initiate activities as often as the staff' (Siraj-Blatchford *et al.*, 2002).

The research team drilled down further to consider what it was that practitioners did that made the difference. Their findings showed that good outcomes for children were linked to the ways in which adults interacted with children during activities. When adult and child are equally involved together, and 'where each party engages with the understanding of the other', working together collaboratively in what is called 'co-construction', then children's thinking is likely to be extended. To do this practitioners need to be able to 'enter the child's world, recognise his/her interests, dilemmas and concerns and have a conversation which encourages further thinking' (Dowling, 2005: 9). The REPEY research used the term 'sustained shared thinking' to describe this highly effective type of interaction. They found that not only were there significantly more episodes of this in those settings with the very best outcomes for children, but also that 'freely chosen play activities provided the best opportunities for adults to extend children's thinking' (Dowling, 2005: 9).

This research has been hugely influential in the early years field, not only in guiding government policy, but also in helping practitioners to reflect on their role. However, rather than just referring to child-initiated or adult-led activities, it is more helpful in unpicking the adult role to see these as part of a continuum including four different types of activity. This will help when planning how best to support children's learning by ensuring each of these is available and planning the adult role more effectively. The four types of activity are:

1. play
2. child-initiated activity/experience (something *the child has decided to do*, which is not play)
3. adult-initiated activity/experience (something *the adult makes available* for the child for a particular learning purpose)
4. adult-led activity (where *the adult leads the children* through a structured learning process with a clear learning objective in mind).

For each of these the adult's role and style of interaction in supporting the learning is different, but equally important. In the first two types of activity the child is in control ('child framed') and in the last two the adult is in control ('adult framed'). As we look at these concepts in more detail I will also be referring to an action research project, 'Interacting or Interfering? Oxfordshire

Adult Child Interaction Project', reported on by Julie Fisher (Fisher, 2012). The project involved a small number of practitioners in Oxfordshire schools, researching and developing their own practice.

Play

An environment for play

We need to make sure we are providing the best environment for play to flourish, if children are to learn and develop 'at their highest level' through play. This means a rich and stimulating, calm and uncluttered environment with different types of play to cater for all the children's tastes, curiosity and interests. When children show little interest in certain aspects of the environment, setting up the provision in a different way can prompt new interest. Being flexible, or as Julie Fisher puts it 'light-footed', is essential in supporting play effectively (Fisher, 2012).

Being flexible

At the Stay and Play session in Old Oak Children's Centre, the sandpit had been emptied in order to mend the base as well as replace the sand. On arrival that day several children went to the area, looking surprised. One child asked where the sand was, and **Myrtle**, the teacher, gently explained what had happened, pointing to the bags of new sand that had just arrived. The child investigated some of the large bags, then waited. Although it was not intended to use the area until the base was mended, Myrtle realised the need for flexibility. She found a tray and together they opened the bags and poured the sand in. Several of the children spent the rest of the morning there, with Myrtle and parents supporting them.

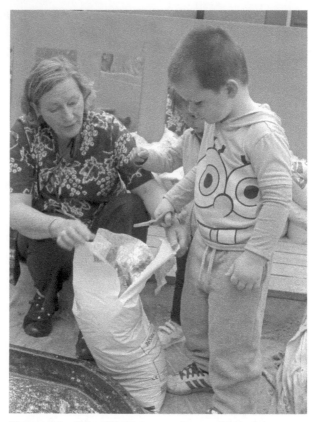

Figure 2.1   Being flexible, responding to children's interests

Adult support

It is entirely the child's choice to play, and the child who leads and controls play, so we have to take care not to take over or interfere. This means sensitively watching and listening: would it help if you joined in, enhancing the play or would it interrupt? Then, if appropriate, ask if you can play then join in sensitively, taking on the role allocated by the child, getting into the pretence (for example, as customer, dog, baby, sister). Stick to the child's theme, rules and flow of the play.

Getting sensitively involved at the right time means that the adult is able to:

- provide language support, by being a conversation partner, sensitively introduce new vocabulary or ways of saying things, through describing or commenting – remember, no closed questions!
- support a child new to the setting or a child who is finding it difficult to get involved in the play
- introduce a new way of doing something, but only if it is consistent with the play – but be prepared for it to be rejected!

Child-initiated activities

Setting up the environment

For an activity or experience to be child initiated, the child must choose to do it and, like play, it should be 'child framed'. However, the many explorations and investigations young children set about doing that are child initiated, highly motivating and deeply involving are more likely to be described by the child as 'work' rather than 'play'. The learning environment inside and outside is a priority. There is a need for novelty as well as the familiar things to explore and plenty of time to do it, with time organised so that children can return to continue their explorations.

Adult support

This is where the adult role is so vital in extending and enhancing children's thinking, supporting creativity and critical thinking. But, as Julie Fisher points out, 'In child led situations, the adult approaches the play not knowing what it is that the child or children are trying to do or what situation they are creating. Child led learning is often spontaneous and frequently unpredictable' (Fisher, 2012). This means watching and listening before getting involved.

Figure 2.2 Getting alongside child-initiated learning, giving sensitive support and encouragement

Getting alongside the children as a fellow 'investigator' in a joint enquiry, sometimes commenting or asking open questions, results in effective support. In this way you are offering your assistance while giving the children space to create and think for themselves. But we need to beware. As Julie Fisher notes in the Oxfordshire project, 'in the early stages of the project, it was clear that adults interfered too much in child-led learning and possibly didn't interfere enough in adult led learning'. In child-led learning the adults 'talked too much' and were 'in danger of hijacking the child's agenda with endless questions' (Fisher, 2012).

Anna Craft talks about the importance of what she calls 'possibility thinking'. 'Fostering children's possibility thinking can be seen as building their resilience and confidence and reinforcing their capabilities as confident explorers, meaning-makers and decision-makers' (Craft, 2007). In 'Finding and Exploring

Children's Fascinations' (National Strategies, 2010) the authors show how Craft's work has important implications for the adult's role, particularly pertinent to supporting child-initiated activity. Using open questions, we can encourage children to take risks, rise to new challenges, be willing to share and make mistakes, as well as be innovative and imaginative. The authors suggest some useful questions:

- Shall we see what happens if ...?
- I don't know how to do that – shall we go and find out?
- I've gone wrong here. How can I do it better?
- Can we do it another way?
- Do you remember what happened when we ...?

In this way 'practitioners also model the meta-cognitive skills that children need to adopt if they are to become successful lifelong learners' (National Strategies, 2010: 15).

Talking with children about the learning processes they are using is vital in developing these meta-cognitive skills, using questions such as 'How did you manage that?' or 'What helped you do that?', and talking about their feelings too: 'How did that make you feel?' Such conversations can be used effectively in both child-initiated learning and 'adult-framed' learning. Sharing something about your own learning is also helpful, giving children an insight into how you as an adult think and figure things out. But remember that 'the best conditions for thinking are not tense. They are gentle. They are quiet. They are unrushed. They are stimulating but not competitive. They are encouraging. They are ... both rigorous and nimble' (Kline, 1999: 37).

Adult-initiated activities

Planning and presentation

Adult-initiated activities differ significantly from adult-*led* activities, in which the adult will stay with the activity for its full duration.

Adult-initiated activities are those that the practitioners put out for children, but they will only involve themselves in this from time to time. For much of the time there is likely to be little adult involvement. The adult may have had a clear learning intention for the children and have chosen to present the activity in a particular way, but is only partly in control of what the children do. Without the adult guidance, the child will choose to use it in their own way and may have quite different personal goals.

The activity or experience should be based in the practitioner's detailed knowledge of the children and their current interests and learning. However, it is all too easy to set up things (such as putting out particular construction sets or setting up the sand with particular equipment) with too little thought or planning. As the EYFS guidance 2008 stated, 'Without observation overall planning would simply be based on what we felt was important, fun or interesting (or all three) but it might not necessarily meet the needs of the children in our care.'

Adult support

When adult-initiated activities are engaging and intriguing to the children, we are likely to see children actively learning and thinking. When getting involved, start from what the children are doing and showing interest in, and follow their train of thought, with a few comments on what you see them do.

Choosing the right moment for your intervention is about being sensitive and responsive, leaving time for the child to respond. If they are not showing interest in what you are showing them then focus on what they are doing, making connections between this and other activities and experiences you know they have been involved in.

Adult-led activities

Adult-led activities are just that: planned by the practitioner with a clear idea of what she/he wants the outcomes to be for the children. Many settings call these 'focused activities', where

Figure 2.3 Teaching a skill

the adult is fully involved throughout. The activity should involve first-hand experiences, be challenging, and either present a new skill, knowledge or idea, or consolidate those that the children are developing. It may include the direct teaching of skills, such as using tools or techniques, such as in painting or working with clay, as well as group times for story and songs. It can follow the learning needs of one child or be planned for a group. However, with babies and toddlers, all activities need to be individually attuned to each child, based on responding to what the child is showing interest in or might be interested in.

Planning and presentation

An adult-led group activity needs to be at the right level of under-standing and challenge for the children, flexible enough to enable them to become deeply involved and make the activity 'their own'. The focus needs to be on the process of learning, not the product. It does *not* mean every child going home with the same product, carried out in the same way under adult instruction! A new skill or concept can be taught in any number of ways, so using the children's interests, learning style and curiosity will help with engagement.

So, in planning adult-led activities, several decisions need to be made. Is this what the children need at this point in time? Will it build on what they can already do, and what we have seen in their play and explorations? Will it ignite new interest, fire the imagination and result in new learning? Is it open-ended enough to enable the children to add to it and take from it what they need? Does it allow for deep involvement and for children to follow up over time in their own ways, with and without adult support?

> When planning activities for special events such as festivals there is a temptation for practitioners to plan adult-led activities with a focus on a presentable product rather than on the learning, and a tendency to set up a kind of production 'assembly line'. **Robb**, a reception teacher, dealt with the issue of Mother's Day in a very special way. He asked every child to 'interview' their mother at home about their favourite activities when they were young. Each child reported back and the answers were recorded by the staff. The children then made little books about this, each completely unique. The last page ended with a very individual 'why my mum is so special to me', written by the child or scribed by the staff, as necessary.

Adult support

From the Oxfordshire research, Julie Fisher reported that in adult-led activities adults were sometimes 'scared to "teach" too much', resulting in 'woolly' input. We must not be afraid to teach when the moment is right, but we need to encourage the children's choices and enable them to express their own ideas, so that they are truly active participants. Evaluating the activity at the end is equally important, including the children in the evaluation. With older children (3 to 4 yrs upwards) this can be through directly asking them what they thought and felt about it, what they enjoyed or found interesting, as they become familiar with being asked to review and evaluate what they think they learned. Sharing photographs taken at the time can help children recall the event and the process of learning they were involved in.

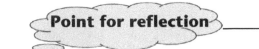

Point for reflection

Consider how the day is planned in your setting: are adults involved in all types of the activities provided and, if so, how? Think about involvement in play, child-initiated activities, adult-initiated activities and adult-led activities.

3   Parents as Partners

In the EYFS Statutory Framework 2012, partnership between practitioners and parents is seen as one of four purposes the EYFS seeks to achieve. But what does this partnership entail? The most important people in children's lives are their parents, intimately involved in every aspect of their care, learning and development. A true partnership with parents means an equal partnership, in which the practitioner and parent share information and work together to support the child's learning and development. This is essential to ensure the child's emotional wellbeing and that s/he settles well into the setting. It involves building the kind of relationship where views and perspectives on how to support the child best can be discussed as well as childcare and child development more generally.

> **Nevaeh**, who is nearly 3, has attended the under threes provision at a Children's Centre since she was 18 months old and her old brother also attended. Ebony, their mother, is very pleased with her and the children's experiences at the nursery: 'The nursery is great – they've done wonders here for me and my children.'
>
> She feels well supported, particularly the way staff have supported her children's emotional wellbeing and happiness, as well as learning and development. This is not accidental; it arises from the setting's deliberate emphasis on partnership with parents, and the professionalism and experience of the staff team in establishing and maintaining it.

An area for development

Most early years settings feel that they have strong and positive relationships with all their parents. Indeed, would a parent allow their child to attend a setting they were not happy with? Developing partnership with parents was raised as a key area for further development in the initial review of the EYFS – the Tickell Review (2011) – although the review noted that 'many settings have adopted their own successful practice to engage parents and carers as partners in their own learning' (Tickell, 2011: 17). This was not the first time the issue has been raised with regard to early years in recent official reports. In 2007, a survey by Ofsted on quality in early years provision noted that 'parents were rarely treated as true partners but, where this did happen, there was a discernible impact on achievement' (Ofsted, 2007).

What are the benefits of parental involvement?

Parental involvement has been seen by successive governments as a way of raising outcomes for those children most at risk of low outcomes as a result of their social and economic status. Over recent years, a wealth of research has shown the benefits of parents and professionals working together, and the importance of parents' involvement in their child's education to outcomes for the children.

The REPEY research mentioned in Chapter 2 also noted the impact of settings with strong partnerships with parents: 'The most effective settings (where outcomes for children were highest) shared child-related information between parents and staff and parents were often involved in decision making about the child's learning programme' (Siraj Blatchford *et al.*, 2002).

In reviewing research on parental involvement in school, Desforges and Abouchaar (2003) found that the factor most influential on children's success at school was what parents did at home with their children. They also found that, in schools with similar intakes, it was those where partnerships with parents were strongest that the children did best. Although the report involved school education the findings are still important to us in the early years.

A further aspect of the EPPE research noted the importance of parents' support for their children's learning at home.

The home learning environment has a greater influence on a child's intellectual and social development than parental occupation, education or income. What parents do is more important than who they are, and a home learning environment that is supportive of learning can counteract the effects of disadvantage in the early years. (Sylva *et al.*, 2007)

Developing strong, supportive relationships

Being inclusive

A respectful environment underpins positive partnerships with parents, where everyone is welcomed and accepted for who they are, their cultures and beliefs acknowledged, respected and celebrated, and no one suffers discrimination. Not only is every child unique but so is every family, and celebrating diversity provides exciting opportunities to broaden perspectives and open minds. Being inclusive requires us to be open-minded, accepting and welcoming to others, celebrating difference as well as looking for and building on our similarities. It involves learning to listen to one another and, in the process, learning to value one another.

Building trust and genuine two-way communication

Building trusting relationships with children is of course a prime responsibility of staff, but so is building trust with parents. Practitioners' perspectives of a child are often very different from the parents', and to support the child best, both perspectives need to be shared. This involves careful listening on the part of the practitioner, taking on board what parents say, enabling them to express their hopes, fears and aspirations about their children. It means being open to their ideas and willing to discuss them, and being aware of potential barriers that can block effective communication.

Recent research by MacNaughton and Hughes (2011) draws on a range of case studies and research in developing partnerships with parents, highlighting the potential for, as well as the actual, unfairness and discrimination. They note the types of practice that can result in 'silencing' parents, such as using jargon, not providing interpreters or not allocating enough time to talk with parents or meet with staff at times that suit them. In these circumstances, it is only the most confident parents who get to talk – often those who are most likely to share the views of the staff. They refer also to 'othering' – when we see ourselves and the way we think as being the norm from which certain others deviate – and 'homogenising' – holding a stereotypical view about people belonging to a particular group, often based on a false premise.

Over recent years in England, Children's Centres have been at the forefront of developing user-friendly services for parents. Many include baby clinics, Health Visitors and other family health-related services, as well as specific programmes and activities around the development of what are called 'parenting skills'. For example, a Stay and Play session, now common in many Children's Centres, provides parents and children with opportunities to play together, facilitated by childcare trained staff. As staff work with both parents and children together, this type of service can provide useful insights into how to work with parents.

The Stay and Play sessions at Old Oak Children's Centre in London provide an important resource for the local parents. There is a core of regular attendees and a constant flow of new joiners. Usually around 30 families attend each session – mother, father or grandmother, with one, two or three children each. The families attending reflect the wide variety of heritages represented in the local community, including Africa, the Caribbean, India, Pakistan, China, Japan, the Middle East, eastern and western Europe, as well as indigenous white Britons.

The three staff – two Children's Centre development workers and the Centre teacher – work hard to make sure everyone feels respected, valued and a full participant in the session, playing alongside the children, talking with the parents about their child, what they are showing interest in, sharing ideas of how to provide support and pointing out the learning they see going on. **Myrtle**, the teacher, said:

> We draw the parents' attention to what their child is doing, explaining what it means in terms of their development and learning. A large part of our role in the sessions is modelling to the parents how best to get involved in the children's play.

Sarah, mother of **Buddy** (aged 2 yrs 2 mths) and **Oakley** (5 mths), has been coming to every session possible since Buddy was a young baby. She told me:

> For me, meeting the other families and mums has been great. It really helps getting to know others with young children. And for Buddy he can do so much here we can't do at home, like the messy play. It's such a different environment and he gets to be with other children.

Another mother agreed with this, and added:

> What has also been important for me has been the opportunity to receive support and advice from the staff too.

Sarah mentioned how important sessions such as 'Cook and Play' have been in helping to broaden Buddy's diet:

> In Cook and Play we made a shepherd's pie with potato on the top and because the children don't just help to cook – cutting up the vegetables, etc. – but we also all eat it together – and Buddy ate it! We cook together at home too – and he loves helping cut up the vegetables. He even ate a piece of raw carrot today.

Building partnerships with every family

The key person plays the greatest role in getting to know the child's parents well, facilitating an open dialogue. There are a range of other strategies too, to support partnership building, such as the regular reviews of the children's progress with parents through one-to-one meetings, events that parents get involved in, and the occasional workshop for parents about an aspect of child development and learning. But let's start at the beginning when a child first joins the setting.

Finding out about the child

Finding out about the child before he/she begins is essential in providing the nurturing environment and ensuring continuity of experience. Start by allowing the parent to tell you what *they* think is important, giving them the opportunity to lead the discussion. Once you have gathered the information they want to tell you, follow-up questions can be asked to fill in the gaps in what you need to know. A list of questions to ask parents is helpful, but the conversations you have with parents are even more important.

Home visits

Many settings carry out home visits before a new child starts in a setting. There are tangible benefits to these, initiating the necessary trusting, positive relationships with child and parent, and helping the settling-in process. But the purpose of the visit must be clear: to begin to get to know the child where she/he feels most at ease.

At Randolph Beresford Children's Centre, the leaflet for parents about home visits states:

> *It will help your child settle more easily if they have met us in their own home; you will be able to tell us everything you want us to know about your child ... We are NOT coming to check on you or assess your child!*

The home visit is carefully planned to ensure an opportunity for the child and key person to begin to get to know each other, time for the parent to find out about the nursery and the staff to find out about the child.

> *We find out as much as possible about the child, their current interests but also the past. For example, if a child was premature this is likely to be significant in their stage of development. We also want to know a bit about the people who are significant in the child's life such as siblings, and other family members. We take some toys with us on the visit, to show the child the kinds of things they can play with at the nursery.*

Informing parents about your setting

These first meetings, whether at a home visit or when the child and parents come to visit, are the time that parents get to know about your setting, its ethos and expectations, as well as practical procedures. Photo displays and photo booklets to take on home visits or have available at meetings can help, but parents may not understand what these are about if they are unfamiliar with play-based learning. It is important to explain the learning taking place in the photos.

Settling in

Settling in to a new setting may mean it is the first time a child has ever been left with anyone other than close family members. This can be very daunting for the parent and the child, and needs sensitive handling and flexibility for both.

The key person role and partnership with parents

The key person is usually the first person that a parent turns to find out how their child has been during the day or over a particular period of time, or if they have queries or concerns. But, as was noted in Chapter 2, the revised EYFS Statutory Framework has strengthened this role to include engaging and supporting parents in 'guiding their child's development at home'. This poses an interesting dilemma as many parents may not welcome being 'told' how to guide their child, and will require support, training and experience to fulfil this well. This is about being open and available to parents, giving *support* when appropriate and sharing ideas when asked.

As the Under Threes Team Leader at Randolph Beresford, Lizzie, said:

> *Parents often ask us for advice especially about behaviour and boundaries which can be very challenging at this age (18 mths to 3). We always share our policy on behaviour management and inform the parents about how we work with the children. We may suggest they might like to try the same approach at home, but it is not our place to challenge parents. They may take a different view from us and respond in a different way, but it is an important discussion.*

Creating a welcoming atmosphere and ethos

It is easy to assume we have created a welcoming atmosphere, but how do you know it will be welcoming to all parents/carers? Greeting parents and the children as they come in is important, and settings with fixed starting times (rather than flexible hours) need to ensure that there is at least one member of staff available to meet and greet, letting parents know of anything special happening that day and directing them to the child's key person.

Displays can help – for example, photo displays of all the children, pegs with children's photos on, family photos in the room at children's heights. Make sure that every child and family is represented – I have visited to settings where a few children have no presence in photos or displays. This is unforgivable! *Be* the ethos you want to create. It is the welcome and inclusiveness that parents/carers, children and visitors receive from you that makes all the difference.

Figure 3.1 This grandmother was an important member of the Forest School outing

Day-to-day communication

The day-to-day professional, working relationship between parents and staff is important; as the EYFS 2008 stated, it is about *being friendly*, not about *being friends* (EYFS, 2008). It means building positive relationships, being prepared to fully share what the child has been doing at home and in the setting. Finding out from parents what the child is doing at home will help the practitioners to tune in to the children more and build on their home experiences, as well as extend the two-way flow of information.'

For many working parents, regular emails and texts, or use of other electronic media, is easier than face-to-face conversations for keeping in contact from day to day, but what about parents whose first language is not English?

Making time and space to talk

Often practitioners say that parents are not interested or don't have time to be involved in the setting. This may well be true, but what attempts have been made? When people think they will have a useful and fulfilling role to play they will find the time, even in busy family and work lives. There are many examples of settings and schools that have developed parental involvement dramatically through a rethink of policy and practice – for example, sharing the child's learning journey with parents and special things their child has done, as well as talking to parents about their own interests. This can lead to them contributing expertise, even if it is only advice through an email on, say, gardening.

Supporting parents to get to know one another

Some settings create a 'buddying' system where parents and families who are more established and know the setting well are asked to pair up with and welcome new families. This seems to work very well, breaking down barriers and apparent 'clique-iness'. It is important to make sure that the parent buddies understand their role is to support the new parents and make them feel welcome. So, ensure that there are clear guidelines for parent buddies so that they know who to go to for more information, or to answer any queries and concerns that may arise.

Parents' evenings and one-to-one meetings

Most settings and schools hold regular parents' evenings, where the child's progress can be discussed. Because evenings may not be the best time for parents, many settings arrange these one-to-one meetings at times that suit the parents best – for example, at either end of the day – planning the dates well in advance so that parents can make plans.

Workshops, outings and social events

Workshop sessions for parents on aspects of child development or to support their understanding of the EYFS can be very valuable. When parents can see a good reason for attending because it is a topic that is important for them and the time of day is right for them, they will attend. Practical strategies that involve the children, such as asking children (over 3) to help make the invitations, also help.

A great way to involve parents is in accompanying children on outings and involving them in special events, such as sharing food at celebrations.

Parental involvement in assessing children's progress

Most settings nowadays create individual learning diaries for each child, openly accessible to parents and the children themselves. These contain the observations, photographs and samples showing the children's learning and development. The best way to involve parents regularly in the assessment process is having the records openly available. Making time for informal conversations about what their child is showing interest in, or skills they are in the process of developing, as well encouraging them to bring in photos or the child's mark making and adding these to the diary, helps these to become a partnership affair, building a fuller picture of the child's real achievements.

> ### Stay and Play: My Learning Journey books, created by practitioners and parents together
>
> At Old Oak Children's Centre Stay and Play the Centre teacher has set up an innovative approach to involve parents as partners in supporting their children's learning, by getting them to document their child's learning and development, with the staff's support, in a Learning Journey booklet. Both parents and staff take photographs and write observations in the sessions when they notice the child do something new or different. There are regular one-to-one discussions with parents about what the child is interested in at home and achievements they have noticed, and parents are asked to bring in their own photos from home. Together a member of the staff team, parent and child add these to the Learning Journey booklet.

The discussions help to draw parents' attention to aspects of their child's development that they may or may not have noticed before, and have in some cases helped them become great observers of their children's development and learning. The booklets are kept in the Centre but frequently go home with the parent and child to show to other family members.

Ben and his mother are looking through his Learning Journey together. This has been a useful opportunity for Ben to reflect on what he has been doing, and a useful, highly relevant context for talk. Referring to a photograph that has taken his interest, the Centre teacher asks Ben: 'Do you remember we planted a potato and some strawberries?'

Ben: 'I planted strawberries and beans.'

There are new photos to add to the Learning Journey and Ben is in charge. He has the glue stick and remembers how the Centre teacher has guided him in how to use the glue on other occasions, like pushing a toy car along the floor. She talks him through it again as he slides the glue stick across the back of the photo: 'Brmm, brmm!'

Figure 3.2 Sharing the child's Learning Journey

Top tips for effective practice

- **Ensure a welcoming and inclusive ethos and environment**, where everyone feels valued.
- **Make time for each key person to talk with parents on a daily basis.** If beginnings and ends of sessions are not convenient for some parents, make sure other channels of communication, such as email, are available.
- **Support parents to get to know one another**, by arranging social events or a parent 'buddy' system.
- **Involve parents fully in the 'record keeping' processes**, as described in the case study box, above.

Points for reflection

What particular actions does your setting take to develop a strong partnership with all parents about their children's learning? Are all parents involved? If so, how? What is in place to help communication between families whose first language is other than English and practitioners? If you are a parent yourself, do you think there is more your child's setting could do?

4   Personal, Social and Emotional Development

A prime area of learning

Personal, Social and Emotional Development (PSED) is the first of the three prime areas of learning and development in the EYFS. The other two prime areas are Communication and Language, and Physical Development. These areas are closely interlinked and of 'prime' importance because they impact on all aspects of life, shaping how children respond to *every* situation. For more information about the differences between the prime and specific areas of learning, turn to the Introduction.

> *Personal, social and emotional development involves helping children to develop a positive sense of themselves, and others; to form positive relationships and develop respect for others; to develop social skills and learn to manage feelings; to understand appropriate behaviour in groups; and to have confidence in their own abilities.* (EYFS Statutory Framework, 2012: 1.6)

How we feel, our ability to relate to others and our self-confidence underpin all learning, but it doesn't just happen. How we, the adults around the children, relate to them makes all the difference between successful and unsuccessful development.

From the very beginning babies are sociable, with an inbuilt drive to *make* others notice them and relate to them. From the moment of birth, babies depend on a close, nurturing relationship with their main carer, usually the mother. This is the beginning of the baby's journey in social and emotional development, affecting self-confidence, ability to manage feelings and make positive relationships with others. Sue Gerhardt's research shows us how the responsiveness of adults close to the baby and the type of care a baby receives is vital in establishing neural pathways in the brain that will set up patterns for the future in how well we cope emotionally through childhood and into adulthood: 'The mystery tonic that enables babies to flourish as soon as they get it, is responsiveness ... not too much (which would swamp the baby, causing stress) and not too little (which would result in stress through neglect) but just the right amount' (Gerhardt, 2004: 196).

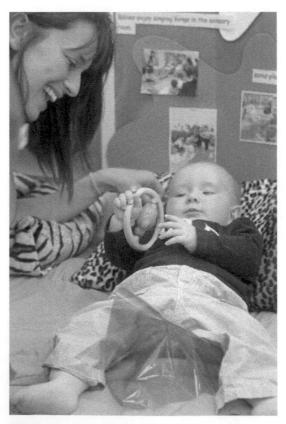

Figure 4.1   Responsiveness is the 'mystery tonic'

In an early years setting, the quality of the relationships between the practitioners and all the children, and an ethos of inclusion, is vital in ensuring children's wellbeing, development and learning. This is why the role of the key person, discussed in Chapter 2, has been developed and made a requirement. An ethos of inclusion puts children, their individuality and their needs first.

The EYFS divides PSED into three aspects, although each is closely interconnected with the others:

1. Making Relationships
2. Self-confidence and Self-awareness
3. Managing Feelings and Behaviour.

Planning for PSED

As PSED permeates all aspects of learning and development it is all too easy to assume that it does not need consciously planning for. Yet providing adult-led activities as well as getting alongside children as they play is important in ensuring all children get the support they need in PSED. The learning environment we set up is also key to whether or not we are providing the best support for the children in all aspects of PSED.

Thinking about the learning environment

A learning environment that is in tune with the interests, learning styles and learning needs of the children becomes an environment that will motivate and enthuse the children to try things out for themselves and take sensible risks. An environment in which the organisation of the day allows plenty of time for informal con-versations between practitioners and children about what the children are doing, the resources they may want to use and what they want to do, will help to develop positive relationships and self-awareness.

The organisation of the environment will also make a big difference to children's behaviour – for example, creating small, calm spaces, inside and outside, where a pair of children or small group can play together uninterrupted by others is important, as are areas for more boisterous play.

Making Relationships

The Early Learning Goal for Making Relationships is the expectation for children at the very end of the reception year, when most will be aged 5.

> *Children play co-operatively, taking turns with others. They take account of one another's ideas about how to organise their activity. They show sensitivity to others' needs and feelings, and form positive relationships with adults and other children.* (EYFS, 2012)

Attending a setting or school usually means that this is the first time a child will be with a group of children of a similar age to themselves, and with adults they do not know well. But every child is different, bringing with them a different set of previous experiences. Some will have had few opportunities to be with and play with other children, others will have had many. A carefully planned settling-in process when the child first starts is essential, flexibly implemented to accommodate each child's personal need for emotional security. Every child is different in this respect, some taking much longer than others to feel confident, settled and ready to make new relationships.

When given the opportunity, such as attending a setting, babies usually show a lot of interest in other babies and young children, and will happily relate to each other for short periods. As they grow and develop they usually want to play with other children, at first playing alongside others, showing interest in what they are doing and beginning to play with others cooperatively. Cooperating with others for a sustained period develops with experience but also depends on confidence and personality. Most children will be highly motivated to spend more time in cooperative, collaborative play with others, but this makes play far more challenging. As Gordon

Figure 4.2 Two year olds playing alongside each other

Wells puts it, 'One of the striking characteristics of such play is how much of the time is spent in negotiating roles and appropriate actions, with the result – in some cases – that there is no time actually left to put the decisions into effect!' (Wells, 1987: 198). But children will sometimes need the sensitive support of an adult or older child to become fully involved and make relationships.

Developing Self-confidence and Self-awareness

The Early Learning Goal for developing Self-confidence and Self-awareness expects that children will be, by the end of the reception year:

> *confident to try new activities, and say why they like some activities more than others. They are confident to speak in a familiar group, will talk about their ideas, and will choose the resources they need for their chosen activities. They say when they do or don't need help.* (EYFS, 2012)

This Early Learning Goal includes as much about talking as it does about confidence and self-awareness, but this is the statement for children at the very end of the EYFS, before they move into Year 1 at school. Being able to communicate their own ideas and communicate when they need help is important for all children at this age, but it develops throughout the child's early years as a result of the support she/he receives.

In this aspect of PSED we can see close links with some of the Characteristics of Effective Learning described in Chapter 1, particularly in 'being willing to have a go', 'keeping on trying' and 'choosing ways to do things'. These rely on self-confidence and self-awareness. How we feel about ourselves has an enormous impact on our ability to learn. Children (and adults) cannot learn in situations where they feel insecure or stressed. As the work of Carol Dweck has shown us (see Chapter 1), the sensitive support adults give to babies and children helps to build confidence and a can-do attitude. This is immensely important. The role of the key person in developing a child's self-confidence is central, ensuring that emotional wellbeing remains high and the child feels able to take on new challenges from the secure base of a supportive relationship.

Positive relationships

With babies, toddlers and young children, so much is learned from the body language, gestures, facial expressions and tone of voice of the adults around them. Long before children understand the words spoken to them, they have picked up strong messages of approval or disapproval about themselves and their actions. This will affect how they feel about themselves and how they act. A child who is insecure, feeling disapproval from others and lacking in self-confidence may be upset and angry, or appear quiet, shy and introverted. Talking sensitively with children, partnering them in some of the activities provided, giving focused praise and being open about one's own feelings will help children develop awareness of their own achievements, boosting confidence.

Assessing emotional wellbeing

To ensure we are doing the best for the children a helpful monitoring tool has been developed by Ferre Laevers, whose work was mentioned in Chapter 1. This is based on assessing children's emotional wellbeing, using a five-point scale. It involves making short observations on the children, looking for signals that demonstrate their level of emotional wellbeing, such as vitality, openness and receptiveness, being relaxed and 'like a fish in water', or at the other extreme, signs of discomfort and tension (Laevers, 2000). It is a very helpful, easy-to-use self-evaluation tool employed in many settings throughout the UK and worldwide. Once the assessments have been made on all the children, action is taken to support any child whose wellbeing appears low. This may mean adjusting the learning environment or changing the way staff interact with the child, providing additional emotional support.

Managing Feelings and Behaviour

The Early Learning Goal for children at the end of the reception year in this aspect of PSED states:

> *Children talk about how they and others show feelings, talk about their own and others' behaviour, and its consequences, and know that some behaviour is unacceptable. They work as part of a group or class, and understand and follow the rules. They adjust their behaviour to different situations, and take changes of routine in their stride.* (EYFS, 2012)

This may seem like a tall order bearing in mind the age of the children, but with thoughtful support throughout the EYFS years, close links with parents, and an ethos and environment in the setting where all children are welcome, feel fully included and supported, it is achievable! There is a tendency to take it for granted that young children will be able to behave in socially acceptable ways, just by being told to 'behave'. However they learn how to manage their feelings through our support and find out about what is acceptable behaviour through the way that adults around them behave. It is important to remember that they learn from *everything* we do, whether we intend this or not.

Feelings and emotions run high in babies and young children, and strong feelings are urgent and sometimes frightening. Children require our support and attention to help them understand and cope with these feelings. Consistency of approach in helping children to manage their feelings and behaviour is important, so regular discussions with parents, planning the strategies of support for the child together is a key to success.

Daily routines can help or hinder the children's concentration, involvement and behaviour. Certain times of day, such as group time, tidy-up time or meal times, may be stressful, especially when the children are required to stop their self-initiated activities. We need to ensure that routines flow with the children's needs rather than for the convenience of the staff.

All children are bound, from time to time, to clash with others, whether verbally or physically. A mother of a 2-year-old child at nursery explains the importance of parents and practitioners working together to support the child:

> She was biting her brother a bit at home, but not as much as she was biting in nursery. I think it was because she wasn't able to get her words across or perhaps just not wanting to say what was upsetting her, but she started to bite her brother. At this time she was around just 2. He is just 18 months older. I talked to her about it but his response was to bite her back!
>
> In discussion with the nursery staff we decided that the best approach was to make it clearer to her – to have it out in front of her – about what teeth were for and make her a bit more conscious about it by talking about teeth and providing her with more appropriate things to bite rather than her friends. Doing the same things at nursery and at home with her really helped, so did talking about what teeth are for.

Julian Grenier (1999) provides a useful example of helping children understand how their own behaviour might hurt others. In the example a child pushes another child over and the key person:

- encourages the child to understand the impact of his behaviour and empathise with the hurt child
- clarifies that the child has crossed a boundary of acceptable behaviour
- spells out clearly the immediate consequence for the child (for example, losing some of his freedom to play for a few minutes).

As Grenier points out: 'The member of staff has not asked "Why did you do that?" – a question that, as a four year-old, he is not developmentally able to answer. Nor has she demanded a formal apology, which may be grudging and insincere' (Grenier, 1999).

Ensuring inclusion: Persona Dolls (for children from 3 yrs upwards)

In Development Matters 2012, in the sections on PSED and Understanding the World, you will find references to Persona Dolls. The Persona Doll approach uses special dolls to tell stories. The dolls reflect diversity so they are made with a range of 'skin' colours, and can also have aids such as glasses or a wheelchair. The aim of the approach is to help the children develop empathy for others, and they provide an effective, easy-to-use way to raise issues of fairness, equality, valuing difference and diversity. The practitioner first creates a personality, family and cultural background for the doll.

To tell the stories, the practitioner sits the doll on her/his lap and, through the stories the practitioner creates, the children find out about the doll and his or her life. The children easily slip into the magic of storytelling and treat the dolls as real people. The practitioner could tell a Persona Doll story one day about the doll going to a birthday party and having fun, and on another occasion tell a story about another child excluding her/him from a game because of her/his skin colour, gender or disability, for example. The 'doll' (through the practitioner) then asks the children what the doll could do to solve the problem, and the children come up with the answers.

By presenting a range of scenarios and problems for children to assess, explore and solve, the Dolls through the stories they tell, open up a world of possibilities and encourage children to imagine what it might be like to live through situations that they have not personally experienced. (Brown, 2008: 22)

Figure 4.3   Using a Persona Doll

Top tips for effective practice

- **Ensure that all children** have supportive and close relationships with their key person.
- **Help children develop relationships** with others by being available when children need this support, getting involved in the activity or play alongside the children.
- **Provide activities that require children to work or play together**, such as outdoor equipment that requires two children to operate it.
- **Observe children's emotional wellbeing** and take action where this is low.
- **Support children to try out new things.** Being a 'learner' alongside the child will show them that you are trying new things too.
- **Talk with children about their feelings**, giving them the vocabulary they need to express them.
- **Talk with children about their achievements** and the processes they used to get there, building awareness of their own learning.
- **For children who need additional support** in managing their feelings and behaviour, observe to find out what triggers the unacceptable behaviour. Taking action to remove the trigger will mean that support is likely to be more effective.
- **Involve children in making the rules for positive behaviour**, helping them to take ownership of the rules.

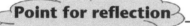

Point for reflection

Make a list, preferably with colleagues from your setting, of all the ways your setting helps children to develop these social and emotional skills. Looking at the 'Top tips for effective practice' section, is there anything more you personally or your setting could be doing?

5 Communication and Language

Communication and language development involves giving children opportunities to experience a rich language environment; to develop their confidence and skills in expressing themselves; and to speak and listen in a range of situations. (EYFS, 2012: 1.6)

Communication and language begin to develop before birth and, by the time a baby is born, she/he is already tuned in to and can recognise her/his mother's voice. Communication and language are essential tools for life: we cannot function independently without them. They include signing and all the various ways we communicate with one another non-verbally as well as verbally, such as through facial expression, body language and gesture.

As a fundamental aspect of child development, the revised EYFS has made it a 'prime' area of learning and development. Communicating is a social activity – there is always more than one person involved. It is thus closely tied to children's social development as well as one of the main vehicles for learning about everything else. As Gordon Wells says, children 'talk to achieve other ends: to share their interests in the world around them, to obtain things they want, to get others to help them, to participate in the activities of the grown up world, to learn how to do things and why things are as they are, or just remain in touch' (Wells, 1987: 53).

Communication and language is divided into three aspects:

1. Listening and Attention
2. Understanding
3. Speaking.

Figure 5.1 Talking together about what interests the child is vital in supporting language development.

These describe the different sets of skills children will need to become adept communicators. Dividing the area of learning and development in this way is helpful, to ensure we do not focus only on speaking – the element most easy to assess.

Children's language and communication development doesn't just develop automatically, it is dependent on what we do as adults to support this development. From the moment of birth, how we use language and communicate acts as their model for focusing attention, understanding and speaking.

A new area of learning and development

Communication and language became an area of learning in its own right in the EYFS in 2012. Before that, in England it was always combined with literacy, resulting in too little emphasis on the importance of language development for all other learning and what adults need to do to support children's development in this key area. However, this change to separate communication and language from literacy does not lessen the link between them.

Books and stories remain as important as ever for language development, from the youngest baby onwards. They remain one of the richest resources for both communication and language *and* literacy development, whether this is looking at books, talking about a book together, or listening to an adult reading. They provide ideal opportunities to experience the rhythm and flow of language, learn new vocabulary and ways of saying things, as well as develop imagination, thought and knowledge.

Listening and Attention

For the Listening and Attention Early Learning Goal, the expectation for children at the end of the reception year, when most will be aged 5, is as follows:

> *Children listen attentively in a range of situations. They listen to stories, accurately anticipating key events and respond to what they hear with relevant comments, questions or actions. They give their attention to what others say and respond appropriately, while engaged in another activity.* (EYFS, 2012)

From the earliest moments in a child's life there is a strong drive to communicate and to be communicated with. In this, eye contact is as important as making sounds and hearing sounds and, for much of the time, it is the baby who initiates the communication, through a cry, smile or coo, and the adult who responds. So it is *the adult* who is initially doing the focused, attentive listening! The two-way process of effective communication is described by Malloch and Trevarthen (2009) as 'proto-conversations', where mother and baby participate in the same rhythm, as in music. It begins at a very young age: a few weeks old.

Assuming the child has no hearing impairment, he/she is not just watching for signs but also listening, distinguishing between different intonations and sounds, and those she/he recognises and others. There is a developmental sequence in listening and giving attention, and in the early stages, attention may be fleeting and the dominant sounds receive the attention. By 12 months infants will usually respond to their own name by turning to look at whoever spoke.

The young child's attention is usually 'single channelled' and the child is unlikely to be able to do one thing, while listening to another. The more we tune in and make our talk what the child is focusing on, the more likely a younger child is to be attentive and listen. When you want the child to change focus, saying the child's name first will help, and then ensuring what you say is at the right level of understanding. This way they are more likely to switch their attention.

Understanding

The Early Learning Goal for Understanding for children at the end of the reception year is:

> *Children follow instructions involving several ideas or actions. They answer 'how' and 'why' questions about their experiences and in response to stories or events.* (EYFS, 2012)

It is not always easy to tell if a child has understood the words we say as, often, they can assume the meaning from the context, or our non-verbal language such as gesture and expression. Pitching our language when we speak to the children at just the right level of understanding is essential for supporting their 'receptive' language (understanding). In the early stages, the language needs to be in the context of the here and now, providing the words in a meaningful context, perhaps naming an object while pointing to it or the action you or the child is undertaking will help, moving on to short, two- to three-word phrases when the child can understand more.

Speaking

The Early Learning Goal for Speaking is:

> *Children express themselves effectively, showing awareness of listeners' needs. They use past, present and future forms accurately when talking about events that have happened or are to happen in the future. They develop their own narratives and explanations by connecting ideas or events.* (EYFS, 2012)

We help children to develop 'expressive' language (speaking) by being good listeners and giving our attention to what they are doing or showing interest in. 'Motherese' is the term given to the type of speech most adults tend to use with babies and infants, supporting all three aspects of language development. In this we emphasise key words with an exaggerated tone and pitch, playfully repeating words and sounds, and simplifying what we say to the right level. It is highly effective as it helps ensure that what we say is at the right level for the child. The optimum level is just a little beyond the child's current level of communication – for example, a child able to communicate using one word may mean that the adult should use just two words.

> Talking with young children is very much like playing ball with them. What the adult has to do for the game to be successful is, first, to ensure the child is ready, with arms cupped, to catch the ball. Then the ball must be thrown gently and accurately so that it lands squarely in the child's arms. When it is the child's turn to throw, the adult must be prepared to run wherever it goes and bring it back to where the child really intended it to go. (Wells, 1987: 50)

The language environment we create for children is important, with plenty to want to talk about, encouragement to do so and plenty of time. With babies and young toddlers, turn-taking

Figure 5.2

games, such as peek-a-boo, as well as singing rhymes and songs many, many times gives plenty of time for repetition. As speech develops and children are moving on from single words to put two or three words together, usually by the age of 2, we can see that not only is vocabulary growing at a fast pace, but the children are picking up the rules of grammar. You will often hear children of 3 and 4 yrs (in English) saying 'I eated it' instead of 'I ate', showing that they have understood the rule about adding 'ed' to express the past tense, but are not yet aware of English irregular verbs.

Children learning English as an Additional Language

Many young children across the UK are learning English as an Additional Language (EAL) and becoming bi- or even multi-lingual. 'Some estimates suggest that as much as two-thirds of the world's population speak more than one language' (National Strategies, 2008: 53).

Being bi- or multi-lingual has many vital benefits for children, not just social (being able to talk with other family members and with others speaking the same language(s) in the wider language community), but it also has a positive impact on cognitive development. The importance of encouraging parents to support their children to become fluent in their first language(s) cannot be overestimated. And, as the authors of the above guidance document pointed out:

> Early Years settings should create a culture that values and celebrates the languages spoken by children. In doing so they will not only support the speech, language and communication development of children learning English as an Additional Language, but will enrich the experience of all children within their setting. (National Strategies, 2008: 53)

Learning an additional language follows a similar pattern in many ways to learning the first language or mother tongue, particularly when the child is immersed in a context where the language to be learned is spoken. For children who are beginning to learn English when they come to your setting, they will already have developed in their first language and will be drawing on their experience, knowledge and skills. But there are differences, too. Often, young children learning the new language will go through what we call a 'silent period', when they are not yet confident to speak in the new language. Much of this has to do with confidence, but it is perfectly natural and the child's understanding of the new language is usually in advance of speaking. The important point here is to ensure that the child is fully involved in all that is going on, through offering sensitive support and making the meaning of what you say clear.

Assessing Communication and Language

For those working in the reception year, it is important to note that, for the Early Years Foundation Stage Profile, the statutory assessment at the end of the EYFS, in Communication and Language, and in Literacy too, children need to be assessed in English. If the ongoing observations and interactions of the children indicate that they are not yet at the expected level in English, they cannot yet be said to have achieved these specific Early Learning Goals. In all the other goals, they can be assessed in their first language.

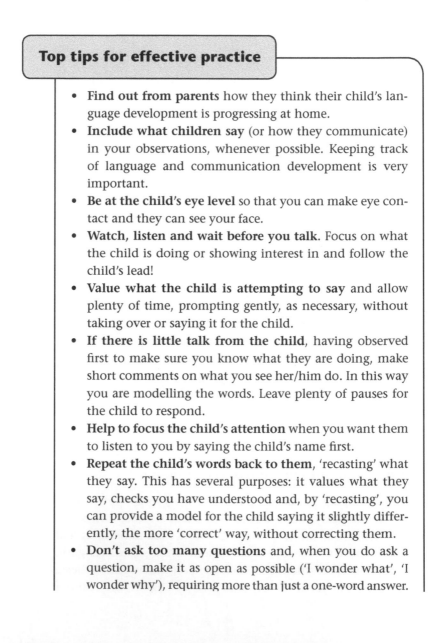

Top tips for effective practice

- **Find out from parents** how they think their child's language development is progressing at home.
- **Include what children say** (or how they communicate) in your observations, whenever possible. Keeping track of language and communication development is very important.
- **Be at the child's eye level** so that you can make eye contact and they can see your face.
- **Watch, listen and wait before you talk.** Focus on what the child is doing or showing interest in and follow the child's lead!
- **Value what the child is attempting to say** and allow plenty of time, prompting gently, as necessary, without taking over or saying it for the child.
- **If there is little talk from the child**, having observed first to make sure you know what they are doing, make short comments on what you see her/him do. In this way you are modelling the words. Leave plenty of pauses for the child to respond.
- **Help to focus the child's attention** when you want them to listen to you by saying the child's name first.
- **Repeat the child's words back to them**, 'recasting' what they say. This has several purposes: it values what they say, checks you have understood and, by 'recasting', you can provide a model for the child saying it slightly differently, the more 'correct' way, without correcting them.
- **Don't ask too many questions** and, when you do ask a question, make it as open as possible ('I wonder what', 'I wonder why'), requiring more than just a one-word answer.

- **Consider the noise level in your setting.** You can reduce background noise by using screens and fabric drapes and the way you plan the learning environment.
- **Provide time for informal conversations.** Meal and snack times, and in particular the outdoor area, provide lots of opportunities for informal chats. But don't talk too much, don't talk for them, and leave them plenty of time to talk with you!
- **Books, stories read and told**, songs and rhymes provide important models for language. All children need these daily and many times a day.
- **Make plenty of opportunities** for children to talk to one another – and plenty of provocations to talk about!
- **Share ideas with parents** about what they do at home and what you do in the setting to support communication and language development.

Figure 5.3 Provide plenty of time for 3- and 4-year-old children to discuss things together

Supporting children learning EAL

As the following points are in addition to the strategies mentioned in the section about learning English as an Additional Language:

- **Learn some key vocabulary** in the child's first language – this shows the child, parents, and other children and families that you value it.
- **Provide plenty of visual clues** to what you are saying. Make sure children in the 'silent period' are not pressurised to talk – this is only likely to reduce their confidence in 'having a go'.
- **Be a partner to the child**, and so ensure that language does not become a barrier to making friends. Explain to other children that the child speaks another language at home, and name the language.
- **Remember it can be very tiring** learning a new language, so space and time to relax is important.
- **Encourage children to speak** in their first language, where they share a language in common. You can do this by making sure you value and talk about their languages.

Point for reflection

Have you had a meaningful conversation with all the children you are responsible for today? This is particularly important if your setting is open-plan. At the end of each day, think about your key children: which children did you really spend meaningful quality time with, where you could communicate with one another in a meaningful conversation-type exchange? Make a list of those you didn't spend much time with and ensure you make time for them the next day.

6 Physical Development

Physical development involves providing opportunities for young children to be active and interactive; and to develop their coordination, control, and movement. Children must also be helped to understand the importance of physical activity, and to make healthy choices in relation to food. (EYFS, 2012: 1.6)

Like Communication and Language, the revised EYFS 2012 has given a much higher priority than ever before to physical development, by making it a prime area of learning and development. It appears that, in England, we are finally beginning to realise exactly how important Physical Development is to children's later learning. As Sally Goddard Blythe states, 'The body has much to teach the brain' (2004). In designating Physical Development as a prime area, the Tickell Review highlighted the importance of physical activity: 'Experience gained during physical activity promotes brain development as well as strengthening muscles and the cardio-vascular system' (Tickell, 2011: 100).

However, Physical Development is much broader than the brief description that appears in the Statutory Framework of the EYFS. It covers a vast area of child development that is considered highly significant in all the Health Checks on children's development by Health Visitors, including sensory development and balance.

The EYFS asks us as practitioners to help children understand the importance of physical activity. But babies, toddlers and young children are very well aware of this. In my experience, ask any 4 year old about their own achievements and learning, and they will nearly always want to tell you about a physical skill they are mastering. As Cooper and Doherty say, children 'love to be active and delight in trying new physical skills, practising established ones and testing their limits in ingenious ways' (2010: 59). So perhaps this point is really directed at us, the adults around the children, and *our* understanding.

The Tickell Review expressed concern about children's 'sedentary lifestyles at home and in early years settings' (Tickell, 2011: 94). Do we allocate enough time for physical activity, allowing children to move and develop their large muscles in a rich, challenging environment? As Jan White (2008), a specialist in the importance of outdoor play, has said: 'We are designed to move, not to sit still.'

Out of doors is best

Luckily for the children, the revised Statutory Framework 2012 has made outdoor play a requirement for all settings:

> *Providers must provide access to an outdoor play area or, if that is not possible, ensure that outdoor activities are planned and taken on a daily basis (unless circumstances make this inappropriate, for example unsafe weather conditions).* (EYFS, 2012)

Unsafe weather conditions means exactly that: not because it is raining, but, for instance, if there is *exceptionally* high wind. We need to remember the adage from the Nordic countries: 'There is no such thing as bad weather, only bad clothing!'

The revised EYFS divides Physical Development into two aspects:

1.   Moving and Handling
2.   Health and Self-care.

Anyone familiar with the 2008 EYFS and, before that, the Foundation Stage, will recall that one aspect within 'Writing', was 'Handwriting'. However, as this is all about the physical skills of being able to hold writing tools appropriately, and the hand–eye coordination to form letters, it has now been, rightly, incorporated into Physical Development. You will also find that one aspect that was included in PSED previously, 'Self-care' is now also incorporated into Physical Development, too.

Moving and Handling

Moving and handling is the term used in the EYFS for the development of:

- gross motor skills controlling large muscle movements, developing a sense of balance and awareness of the body in space (proprioception)
- and fine motor skills, which include the development of hand–eye coordination, and the hand and finger control and strength that enables us to use tools.

The Early Learning Goal for the end of the reception year, when most children are aged 5 states:

> *Children show good control and co-ordination in large and small movements. They move confidently in a range of ways, safely negotiating space. They handle equipment and tools effectively, including pencils for writing.* (EYFS Statutory Framework, 2012)

Gross motor skills

By the age of 3, when enabled and encouraged, most children have learned to walk, run, climb and make a host of other movements. They can also use their hands to pick up, carry, throw and use some one-handed tools. However, it takes a lot more experience to reach the Early Learning Goal.

Playing outside in plenty of space is hugely significant in giving children the freedom to try things out and experiment

Figure 6.1

with what their bodies can do, through their play and self-initiated activities. They need experience of crawling, climbing, spinning, tilting, tumbling and sliding to develop the balance and skill necessary for more sophisticated movements. Personal confidence is a significant factor in whether children will take risks and try these things out for themselves. So fun, planned activities, such as running and balancing games, opportunities to dance, play at moving like different creatures or try out an inviting obstacle course are also very important in making sure we provide appropriately for children's all-round Physical Development.

Physical Development takes place in a sequential pattern, control of the head before the body and from inner core to outer, beginning with the larger muscles. It is only later on, with good development of the large muscle movements that the fine motor skills and strength, of the hands in particular, develop. Goddard Blythe also makes an important point for those working with young and older children: 'the most advanced level of movement is actually the ability to stay totally still' (Goddard Blythe, 2011: 182).

A sense of balance

Much of the control of movement and physical activity depends on being able to balance. Goddard Blythe (2011) refers to balance and proprioception – our awareness of our body's position in space – as two additional 'internal' senses. It takes lots of practice and plenty of opportunities for a baby (at 7–8 mths) to have enough balance and control to sit up freely without support. Sitting up in a supportive chair may mean that the baby can see what is going on around them, but too much time in this position is not good for developing the strength and control they need. Placing babies on the floor to freely kick their legs and move their arms is important, and especially so that they can spend short periods of time on their tummies. Make sure you give your full attention to the baby, encouraging and chatting to her/him while ensuring she/he is comfortable, stopping when there are signs of discomfort.

Soon they will be moving, either crawling or bottom shuffling (or both), although it may be months before they start to walk without support. Parents often see walking as a really important milestone and are delighted if their child is an early walker. But the

Figure 6.2 Tumbling in the long grass

importance of the skills leading up to walking, such as crawling, which help in developing balance, must not be underestimated: 'What we are coming to realise is that it is not how quickly a child reaches the goal of walking that matters but how effectively they work through these important stages' (O'Connor, 2012).

For all aspects of Physical Development, but particularly for balance and proprioception, rough-and-tumble play is important. It is also important in developing close relationships, knowing about others and how to have physical fun together without hurting one another, assessing risks and understanding safety.

Fine motor skills

It requires a great deal of strength in the hand and fingers to hold and be able to use a pencil or other one-handed tools such as scissors. These fine motor skills will be helped most by providing a wealth of opportunities for children to use their whole bodies for a wide range of movements, their arms as well as legs. Fine motor development is dependent on coordination of the limbs and the coordination of the eyes with the hands. Hand–eye coordination develops with the maturity of the baby so that by a few months old a baby will reach out to grasp an object accurately but still needs strength to manipulate it as intended. It all takes time and maturity as well as experience.

Health and Self-care

Health and self-care in the EYFS is about how we help young children to develop the skills to look after themselves physically, but it is also about developing their understanding about keeping healthy. The Early Learning Goal that children should be able to achieve by the end of the reception year states that:

> *Children know the importance for good health of physical exercise, and a healthy diet, and talk about ways to keep healthy and safe. They manage their own basic hygiene and personal needs successfully, including dressing and going to the toilet independently.* (EYFS, 2012)

As we can see much of this expectation for children at age 5 is about knowledge and being able to communicate it. Children will need plenty of practical experiences and time for discussion in order to achieve this. This means there is a need for us to provide experiences that help them to keep healthy, such as a healthy diet and plenty of exercise out of doors, as well as talking to them about why these are important.

This does not require formal discussions but conversations when children are playing, so that they relate to children's actual bodily experiences, such as talking with them about the changes they feel within their bodies when they run or exercise vigorously, are hot or are cold, and how they balance, as well as the kinds of movements they like best.

> Talking with **Jessica**, aged just 5 yrs and at the end of the reception year, about her achievements, which are captured in her Learning Diary, her handwriting development was an important achievement to her, but as I wrote at the time: 'It was quite clear from her actions afterwards that skipping and hopping at the same time was an important new achievement, which she was busy practising: "I can hop and do it. Look I CAN do it!"' (Hutchin, 2003).

Supporting parents

Sharing ideas with parents about how your setting is supporting their child's Physical Development and what parents do at home will help to ensure continuity of experience for children. It is often helpful to hold workshop sessions for parents about why Physical Development, especially gross motor skill development, is so important and how, for example, gross motor skill helps develop the strength and muscles needed to use tools such as pencils for writing. Parents are also often concerned about their child's diet and about toilet training, such as when and how to potty train, so discussion groups on these topics will be supportive.

Top tips for effective practice

An enormous variety of physical activities and experiences will help babies, toddlers and young children develop their physical skills. And, as always, observing the children is not only important in assessing their skills and confidence, but also in reviewing and reflecting on whether your provision offers the right level of challenge for the children and how effective practitioners are in encouraging and extending children's learning and development.

- **Have fun with the children**, by joining in as they play and by planning a variety of challenging physical experiences.
- **Ensure you set up your environment** creatively to encourage the children to explore and experiment with a range of ways of moving.
- **Give children plenty of time to try things** out for themselves, with time to repeat things as they wish, time and time again.

For babies

- **Make sure small babies** who are not yet sitting do not spend too long in chairs. Allow them to kick and move their arms freely while lying on their tummies.
- **Provide different types of surface** for babies to crawl on; this will offer a range of sensory experiences for legs and hands. As they become walkers let them walk as much as possible with bare feet on different safe surfaces.

For toddlers

- **Provide opportunities** to walk, run, crawl and climb, over, under and through things, to help fine-tune awareness of body in space.

For young children

- **Encourage a wide range of movements** to develop balance and strength.
- **Let children experience rough-and-tumble play** in a safe environment.
- **Create obstacle courses and fun games** to encourage children to use different muscles and different ways of moving. Outside, action rhymes, games and songs on a large scale allow freedom of movement not possible inside.
- **Encourage crawling** as it strengthens the hands, and games using equipment such as bats, balls and beanbags support the development of arm movements.
- **Provide opportunities for dancing**, twirling scarves and ribbons, and using musical instruments.
- **Provide malleable materials** (clay, dough, etc.) without tools so that children can manipulate with their hands: pinching, rolling, pulling, shaping, squashing.
- **Teach children how to hold tools** – sometimes direct teaching will help, but children need plenty of opportunities to practise.
- **Talk with children about their bodies** and the changes that take place while they are involved in being physically active, such as running.
- **Talk to children** about their physical achievements.
- **Grow vegetables and fruit with the children** and, when cooking with the children, make sure your recipes are healthy ones, discussing with them why they are healthy. Help children to know which foods are healthiest, and always provide snacks and meals that are healthy.

Figure 6.3 Providing opportunities for children to challenge themselves physically

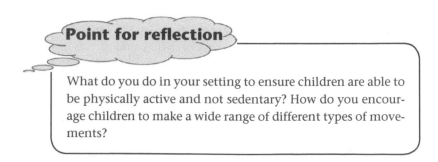

Point for reflection

What do you do in your setting to ensure children are able to be physically active and not sedentary? How do you encourage children to make a wide range of different types of movements?

7   Literacy

Literacy, along with Mathematics, Understanding the World, and Expressive Arts and Design has been designated as a 'specific' area of learning in the revised EYFS 2012. The specific areas are *dependent* on the prime areas we have been discussing in the previous three chapters, and linked to a specific body of knowledge and skills rather than to child development. Literacy is strongly dependent on children's language development and ability to communicate. In the EYFS, literacy is described in the following way:

> *Literacy development involves encouraging children to link sounds and letters and to begin to read and write. Children must be given access to a wide range of reading materials (books, poems, and other written materials) to ignite their interest.* (EYFS, 2012: 1.6)

But literacy involves much more than just the technical skills of linking sounds to letters, and the Statutory Framework just gives us a partial definition of what it takes to learn to read and write. First, children need to know a great deal about spoken language and how it works – and, for example, that the squiggles that we call writing convey a message, and they need to *want* to find out what the message is: 'The complex skills of writing and reading emerge out of children's earliest communications, talking, drawing, encounters with stories and books, and interest in everyday marks and print in the environment' (Whitehead and Thompson, 2010: 157).

The EYFS description of literacy talks about children being 'given access to a wide range of reading materials'. This really means adults reading a rich variety of appropriate materials to young children, enthusing them about the exciting things to be found in books, and the messages conveyed by the print they see around them. As Communication and Language form the roots of literacy, children need rich opportunities to communicate in play and in their daily lives with their peers as well as adults who listen to them well and engage in meaningful conversations with them.

We cannot function effectively in the modern world without being literate: 'Being literate makes all the difference to their chances of social acceptability, worthwhile employment, extended educational opportunities and material success' (Whitehead, 2009: 56). Children take their models of behaviour from the adults around them, particularly from parents and practitioners. Books and stories open doors and transport us to other worlds; they fire the imagination and get us thinking. If we show that we value literacy by giving books and stories a high priority, reading to children frequently and showing that we need to write things down, we are providing good models for young children to follow.

The EYFS 2012 highlights two aspects of literacy:

1. Reading
2. Writing.

Reading

The Early Learning Goal for children at the end of the reception year, when most are aged 5 yrs states:

> *Children read and understand simple sentences. They use phonic knowledge to decode regular words and read them aloud accurately. They also read some common irregular words. They demonstrate understanding when talking with others about what they have read.* (EYFS, 2012)

Being able to read involves two major sets of skills and knowledge:

1. comprehension – understanding the message, the *meaning* that the writing conveys

Figure 7.1

  2. technical de-coding skills – knowing how to de-code
      groups of symbols (words); this depends on the child's
      knowledge of phonics (the sounds our letters make) and
      other knowledge about how written language works.

Both of these aspects depend first on the child developing a rich
vocabulary and understanding of verbal language. Reading is far more
than de-coding the writing, and comprehension is vital – otherwise
decoding the words is pointless! The only way children will develop
a desire to know what the writing means is through adults helping
them to understand that the marks (the writing) have meaning.

Early reading skills

Comprehension

Children need to find out a great deal about writing, books, stories
and reading if they are to become readers themselves. Being given
plenty of opportunities to look at and talk about books, as well
as being read to, is also essential. There is so much to talk about

when sharing a book: discussions about the characters or the storyline, for example, and what is going to happen next. As this conversation takes place, you can begin to draw the child's attention to the writing, pointing out some of the features of the print such as a repeated refrain ('Who's been eating *MY* porridge?'), while running your finger under the words.

Most of these early skills children need in learning to read are listed in Development Matters Guidance, under the 30–50-month age band. Skills such as retelling the story from memory, being able to use the pictures to retell a story, to predict the ending of a sentence because of its meaning, or by finding the right word because it rhymes with another word, are all important skills.

De-coding skills

The first word that children learn to recognise is usually their own name, starting with the first letter. And, once they have done this, finding other children's names that start with the same letter or letter combination as theirs is important, and then picking out other words that start in the same way, too.

Although the EYFS stresses the importance of phonics, children also need to know, for example, that in English, print is read from left to right, that the writing marks are broken into meaningful words, before they are ready to learn about the link between letters and the sounds they make. It is only later on that they will be ready to find out that words are composed of different sounds using letters and groups of letters.

Nursery rhymes and songs are important in helping children's development of speaking and listening as well as reading skills because they help them to understand the patterns of language. The rhythm of our speech helps children to hear the emphasis in speech, and rhyme helps children to focus on similar sound patterns, which helps them to predict what comes next. As well as this, they need to have fun with words that begin with the same sound. This is called alliteration and helps children focus on the beginning of the word.

Learning phonics

Phonics enables us to de-code words by sounding out the parts of words and 'blending' these together to read, or 'segmenting' them to write. Once children are showing interest in letters and words they may be ready to start learning phonics. The smallest letter/sound unit is called a *phoneme* and, although we have 26 letters as there is no simple sound–letter relationship in English, we also have 44 phonemes. For example, S and H make two very different sounds but together make the 'sh' sound.

Most children begin to learn about phonics in the reception class in school. This involves teaching them the phonemes, and blending these together in order to make up words and read them. Children also need to recognise letters and their order in the alphabet, and they also build up a memory of whole words, which helps particularly with reading words that cannot easily be de-coded using phonics.

Writing

As with reading, the writing Early Learning Goal expects a high level of skill for children at the end of the reception year, with an emphasis on phonic skills to help them spell:

> *Children use their phonic knowledge to write words in ways which match their spoken sounds. They also write some irregular common words. They write simple sentences which can be read by themselves and others. Some words are spelt correctly and others are phonetically plausible.* (EYFS, 2012)

However, as with reading skills, there are two sets of skills children need as they learn to write:

1. composition – deciding what to write and composing the message
2. transcription – knowing how to write it.

There are also the physical skills needed to write, which are found under Physical Development. In the Early Learning Goal there is a very clear emphasis only on the transcriptional skills, with no mention of comprehension, the purpose of the writing. But the compositional skills are very important indeed – writing needs a purpose!

Early writing skills: making marks

Although babies make marks deliberately, very early on in life, as they move their hands backwards and forwards, perhaps through spilled food or drink, this early mark making is not related to the type of mark making that later becomes writing.

Composition: the purpose of writing

It is when young children begin to ascribe meaning to their marks that their mark making turns into a deliberate attempt to draw or to write. For some children this may be as young as 2, for others much later, dependent on their experience of being given opportunities to make marks. Watching adults writing provides an important model, especially when they tell the child what they are writing – for example, a shopping list, a telephone message or writing an observation on a child.

Figure 7.2 Elshaddai's writing-like marks

Figure 7.3 Nevaeh's writing

In the examples in Figs 7.2 and 7.3, the children (aged 3 yrs 1 mth and 3 yrs 2 mths), Elshaddai and Nevaeh, had been watching me write and wanted to do some too. Elshaddai's mark making here was very carefully executed, but she did not say what the message was. Nevaeh was less careful but was very clear about the message and, as she points to different parts of her mark making, she tells me: 'That says Mum, that's Joel, Nevaeh.'

One of the best ways of helping children to understand how to compose a message to be written down, and the most powerful model for writing, is scribing something that the child dictates to you, such as a caption they want on their drawing or a message in a card they are making. Like reading, for most children, the first and most important thing they usually want to write is their own name. In the example in Fig 7.4, Emma, aged only 2 yrs 7 mths, is already bringing together both the transcriptional and compositional aspects of writing, as she attempts to write her name on the back of a drawing.

Figure 7.4 Emma has written some letters for her name

Transcription: writing it down

In Fig 7.4, we can see Emma's attempt at writing her own name. She already knows the letters in her name and can recognise it when she sees it written, but forming the letters correctly takes time, even for a child like Emma who loves to make marks and draw, and spends a great deal of time having fun with this at home and at nursery. Lots of exploration and experimentation on a large scale, such as on large paper or outside on the ground, will help.

Linking sounds and letters for writing

When children are ready – usually, but not always, around the age of 5 – they will need adults to support them in learning how to break words up ('segment') into their component parts (phonemes) to write them. A phoneme written down is called a 'grapheme'. As children begin to understand how this link works you will see them quietly sounding out the parts of a word, and thinking about what letters and phonemes to use. This is when they begin to make 'phonetically plausible' attempts at writing words. Some frequently used words, however, they manage well from memory.

Top tips for effective practice

Reading

- **Read to children frequently, from babies onwards.** As you do so, allow plenty of time to look at the book and talk about it. Enjoy it and so will the children!
- **Have an inviting book area** with a range of good-quality books, fiction and non-fiction, poems and rhymes. Make sure there are story props and sacks available, too.

- **Check through the books in your setting regularly:** are they invitingly displayed and in good condition? Do they cater for the children's differing interests? Are the main characters in the stories and books from different cultural and ethnic backgrounds? Do they celebrate ethnic and cultural diversity?
- **Sing rhymes and songs** daily with babies, toddlers and young children. Sing the words as clearly as possible so children understand them.
- **Involve young children in acting out** favourite stories and in making up their own versions.
- **Point out to children** what the words on your displays and notices say, as well as signs they see in the street.
- **Provide alphabet friezes** and alphabet books to help children get to know the letters of the alphabet.
- **Play fun games** with older children, focusing on initial sounds in words, and games where you divide words into phonemes and they have to guess the word. This is suitable for most 4 year olds and some 3 year olds, too.

Writing

Many of the points for effective practice in reading also help to develop writing skills.

- **Give children plenty of reasons** to make meaningful marks in their play, such as shopping lists, registers, messages and appointments.
- **Have clipboards everywhere** to encourage mark making and writing, buckets of water with paintbrushes for outside, as well as chalk and chalkboards.
- **Talk with the children** about their writing-like marks, giving them plenty of time to tell you about what they are doing.
- **Have children's names** written on cards to encourage them to write their own names.

- **Make books with the children** – about the children themselves, their own stories or versions of familiar stories.
- **Scribe** for the children, writing down what they dictate to you. Talk to them about it as you do it.
- **Write in front of the children**, such as the notes, lists and messages you need.

Point for reflection

How often are books shared with children one to one or in a very small group in your setting? Over the course of a week, keep a tally of how often you and other staff read books to small groups of children during the session. Is it always the same children who ask for a story? Note down which children get involved and which don't. How can you encourage children who may be missing out? For example, do you need to find other spaces to read (e.g. outside or in the construction area) or other types of books?

8 Mathematics

In the EYFS, Mathematics is described in the following way:

> *Mathematics involves providing children with opportunities to practise and improve their skills in counting numbers, understanding and using numbers, calculating simple addition and subtraction problems, and to describe shapes, spaces, and measures.* (EYFS, 2012: 1.6)

Recent research has shown that 'beginning formal instruction at an early age does not improve subsequent mathematical achievement' (Evangelou *et al.*, 2009: 43). What young children need to develop mathematical understanding and skills is plenty of first-hand, practical experiences, time to explore new ideas and concepts, encouragement to have a go and confidence to persist.

Mathematical experiences for children start at a very young age. Very young babies look for patterns, explore shapes visually and, soon enough, physically, as they begin to interact with the world around them, using their mouths, hands and whole bodies. Although we may not call this a strictly mathematical exploration, they are nevertheless becoming aware of how shapes feel and how they behave in different ways because of their shapes. Many other early encounters with the world that are primarily social often incorporate an element of number and mathematical calculation – for example, parents may count toes, feet and socks when dressing, share things out ('one for you, one for me') and frequently refer to 'more'.

The EYFS divides mathematics into two aspects:

1. Numbers
2. Shape, Space and Measures.

But mathematics is not *just* about being able to count accurately or knowing the names and properties of simple shapes. As they explore the world around them, and especially in their play, their mathematical skills and knowledge help them to investigate and solve the problems they encounter: 'When mathematical experiences are rooted in children's individual interests and fascinations it increases their engagement, motivation and desire to learn' (National Strategies, 2009a: 15). As we get involved in children's play we introduce them to mathematical vocabulary of number, position, size and shape, just as we do with other vocabulary.

> Children pick up this mathematical vocabulary in the normal course of day to day talk. If we only use words such as 'big' and 'little', rather than 'long/short', 'wide/narrow', 'heavy/light', the children will only learn 'big' and 'little', so we do need to be accurate in the terminology we use. (Hutchin, 2012: 184)

The learning environment

'Children can learn mathematics through play provided there is deliberate, thoughtful planning for and from children's interests, with long uninterrupted periods for them to play' (Carruthers and Worthington, 2011: 172). Ensuring the learning environment indoors and out of doors is full of mathematical potential encourages children to explore in mathematical ways, enabling them to encounter maths in play and self-initiated activities, as well as making it easier for practitioners to introduce adult framed experiences. This does not mean buying expensive equipment, but setting out everyday equipment in a way that will lend itself to children exploring aspects of mathematics. For example, having graded-capacity containers for sand and water play is important, but unless they are displayed and stored as a set children will not see the mathematical potential. Collections of natural materials (conkers, twigs, pebbles, etc.), or objects such as old spoons, buttons or doorknobs,

Figure 8.1   In a rich and well-planned learning environment, any activity can lend itself to maths

provide excellent open-ended mathematical resources to explore, use in play, sort and count – and all free of charge! But, to be of any use, they need to be displayed visibly and organised as collections.

Numbers

The Early Learning Goal for the end of the reception year when most children are 5, states that:

> *Children count reliably with numbers from 1 to 20, place them in order and say which number is one more or one less than*

a given number. Using quantities and objects, they add and
subtract two single-digit numbers and count on or back to find
the answer. They solve problems, including doubling, halving
and sharing. (EYFS, 2012)

Babies hear numbers and vocabulary about quantity from a
very early age, so it is hardly surprising that as soon as they can talk
we often hear them use number names. Although they may not say
the numbers in order, they are often very clear about the kind of
contexts and situations in which to use them. For example, a 2 year
old may say 'one-two-three' for each stair while climbing up the
stairs. Using number rhymes and songs with babies, toddlers and
young children helps them to pick up ideas about what the number
names mean, especially if these are sung or said using props, fingers
or the children themselves as the objects to be counted.

Young children have their *personal numbers* and the first of
these is their own age: how often do you hear children say 'I'm 4'
when you are in the midst of counting. Other personal numbers
may be the ages of their siblings, or the number on the front door.
They also love the idea of very large numbers. For example, Maya,
aged 4 yrs 2 mths, said, looking at her collection of small shells,
'I've got loads here.' Rosie replied: 'And I've got 300. That's zillions!'

Counting

Children spend a significant amount of time moving towards
counting before they have understood the concept of counting and
mastered the necessary skills. To be able to count children need to:

- know some number names
- know there is a correct order for numbers that does not
  vary
- understand that there must be one-to-one correspondence between the number name and the object being
  counted, even if the object cannot be seen
- make the necessary one-to-one correspondence.

We help children to get to this stage by providing plenty of real experiences, counting with them, pointing to the objects and, in the process, modelling how to do it. Number books, full of fun and humour, also provide a great context for learning to count.

Recognising numerals

Providing number friezes and using numerals purposefully, both indoors and outside, will help children to become familiar with what they stand for. Opportunities for using numerals can be everywhere in the learning environment, such as labelling the storage pots of tools (4 scissors, 8 pencils, etc.) and, outside, creating numbered parking spaces for the wheel toys that correspond to the toys themselves. This not only raises children's awareness of numerals but gives them purposes for counting – and helps with tidying up and care of resources.

Making mathematical marks

Given the opportunity, children will develop their own ways of representing numbers and other mathematical ideas in their play and child-initiated activities. In this way they are applying what they already know and extending it to new situations – for example, making tickets for turns on the wheel toys, or the seat numbers for the imaginary bus. For this we need to provide the appropriate mark-making equipment in all the places that children might want to use it, inside and outside, such as clipboards and chalk for chalking on the ground.

Solving problems and calculating

'When problems arise from contexts that are personally meaningful and relevant to the children, their curiosity is sparked and they are likely to be highly motivated' (National Strategies, 2009a: 27). In a preschool, nursery or school setting, practitioners use calculation all the time throughout the day: knowing how many children of the full 'set' are staying for lunch and therefore how many places to set at the table, or cutting up fruit for snack (a great opportunity to use words such as 'half' and 'quarter') are just two examples. These daily routines can provide some of the best opportunities to involve children in meaningful adult-framed mathematical experiences that they will then use in their own explorations, investigations and play.

Number rhymes and songs are very effective in helping children to both add and take away, but most of our well-known songs only include numbers to five and nearly all take away. Look out for those that add and count forwards, and when you think the children are ready, increase the number beyond five. Games also provide ideal opportunities to count and calculate for real purpose: both board games and active games outside, such as skittles.

Practitioners need to take an 'investigatory' approach, thinking aloud and asking open-ended questions. For example, getting children to help set the tables for lunch, the practitioner can ask: 'I wonder how many children we should put at each table today?'

Figure 8.2 Counting the cups for hot chocolate at Forest School

This will become a meaningful problem-solving activity about the shape of the tables and the number of chairs it is possible to get around each table. Carruthers and Worthington (2010) point out, too, that the problems to solve are the ones the children choose, rather than the ones we as adults impose on them.

Shape, Space and Measures

The Early Learning Goal for Shape, Space and Measures expects that, by the end of the reception year, children will be able to:

> *use everyday language to talk about size, weight, capacity, position, distance, time and money to compare quantities and objects and to solve problems. They recognise, create and describe patterns. They explore characteristics of everyday objects and shapes and use mathematical language to describe them.* (EYFS, 2012)

First-hand experiences of objects of different shapes, dimensions and weight are essential in understanding shape, space and the need for measurement. Providing opportunities for exploring natural materials is important, such as those put in a 'Treasure Basket' for babies. As babies explore the objects in the basket they will be experiencing the different 'mathematical' properties of the objects – such as weight, whether it has corners, is spherical or cylindrical – using all their senses. Soon they become interested in what they can do with these objects and how they work – for example, a spherical object such as a ball may roll away but cannot be piled up, whereas bricks can be piled up and knocked down. Such experiences bring together aspects of early Mathematics, Understanding the World, and Expressive Art and Design.

Although children's earliest encounters with the world of mathematics are through developing awareness of pattern, shape and space, and we enable them to explore these, it is not until later on that we really begin to talk about it with the children. This does not mean giving lessons in how to name the objects, but using the naming vocabulary in context and asking the children open-ended questions relating to what they are attempting to do.

Play out of doors can provide mathematical experiences through role play, fantasy play and generally exploring the environment – for example, noticing the patterns of the paving stones or bricks in the wall. Everything can be on a larger scale than inside. Block play is particularly helpful for developing awareness of shape and the properties of shape. Allowing plenty of time and encouragement to explore, build, knock down and rebuild with sets of blocks of different shapes is important. Role play and fantasy will need particular spaces and props to be created, involving children in measuring and understanding shape. With practitioners as play partners, there can be many useful conversations about Shape, Space and Measures.

Top tips for effective practice

- **Support parents** to understand that mathematics is not just about sums. As well as Informal conversations, running an 'open afternoon' for parents can demonstrate how maths can be an aspect of every play opportunity.
- **Look carefully** at your resources, and particularly how they are stored and displayed. Do they enable children to see the mathematical potential?
- **Use every opportunity available** to take a problem-solving approach, talking with children about their own ideas and supporting them in following these through their own investigations as well as real purposes you might have.
- **Help children to problem solve** when issues involving sharing and taking turns arise, as these can be ideal for mathematical thinking.

- **Make tidy-up time** an exciting mathematical experience and, when possible, involve children in the setting up of activities, too.
- **Encourage children's mathematical mark making** by making the necessary tools and equipment in every area and encouraging them to make their own representations.
- **Sing plenty of number songs and rhymes**, and act them out with the children.
- **Use books and stories** to provide the basis for mathematical activities. Traditional tales are particularly good for this, but also make up your own versions and encourage the children to do the same.
- **Play all sorts of games** – active games outside or board games inside.
- **Provide Treasure Baskets for sitting babies**, but remember that toddlers and young children love these, too.
- **Get involved in children's block play and construction play**, as a play partner.
- **Find opportunities to measure things** in real situations for real purposes.

Cooking can provide great opportunities for counting and measuring, and other areas of learning and development. However, cooking such as baking cakes usually requires very specific quantities and procedures, and may require the children to just follow the adult's directions. Make sure that children are given opportunities to explore and experiment, too. Making dishes such as fruit salad or soup can be more flexible and just as useful for mathematical learning. Creating your own recipe cards with simple, illustrated instructions, with one instruction per page, can provide very good support for children to follow a particular sequence.

Point for reflection

How many opportunities are there for mathematical experiences in your outdoor area? Are your resources organised in such a way that children can see the mathematical potential? Are there collections of natural materials (stones, pebbles, twigs, etc.)? Are children encouraged to collect these, too? Are there tools such as measuring sticks and numerals that children can move and use? How is the role play area outside organised, and how many maths opportunities are there here? Are there opportunities for children for mark making – for example, developing chalking on the ground or painting with water?

9   Understanding the World

The revised EYFS describes Understanding the World, a specific area of learning, in the following way:

> *Understanding the world involves guiding children to make sense of their physical world and their community through opportunities to explore, observe and find out about people, places, technology and the environment.* (EYFS, 2012: 1.6)

It covers a vast area of children's learning about the human world as well as about the environment and everything within it. As the title acknowledges, it is largely about developing children's *understanding*, and there is far less emphasis on skills than we find in Literacy and Mathematics. In the process of their learning about the world, babies, toddlers and young children apply all of the Characteristics of Effective Learning (see Chapter 1). With our help, as they make sense of the world around them, they will become deeply involved in observing, exploring, asking questions, finding answers and reflecting about what they find out.

Understanding the World is divided into three aspects:

1.   People and Communities
2.   The World
3.   Technology.

The first two are seamlessly interconnected with the prime areas of learning, as children experience and find out about the 'human' world through their relationships and interactions with others (PSED, and Communication and Language). It is from this that they branch out and explore the wider world using all their senses and the physical skills they are developing. Other specific areas of learning and development play an important part in

Figure 9.1 Daisy, aged 3 yrs 3 mths: stars and shooting stars – 'The dots are stars and where there's tails, they're shooting stars'

Understanding the World, too, as children find ways to communicate through talk, reading and writing, apply their skills in counting, classifying and solving problems, as well as represent their experiences creatively. The third aspect refers to children becoming familiar with and using a range of technology.

People and Communities

The Early Learning Goal for children at the end of the reception year, when most children are 5, is as follows:

> *Children talk about past and present events in their own lives and in the lives of family members. They know that other children don't always enjoy the same things, and are sensitive to this. They know about similarities and differences between themselves and others, and among families, communities and traditions.* (EYFS, 2012)

Starting from the child

This aspect of learning and development starts with the child's personal sense of history through remembering personal events. But the next two sentences in the Early Learning Goal make us think about what we are doing to support children to become aware of others, and the similarities and differences between themselves and others, as well as helping them develop understanding of the local and wider community. It is closely linked with the preparation and provision we make for children's Personal, Social and Emotional Development as we support them to develop positive relationships with others and understand their own and others' feelings. It depends on creating an inclusive ethos in the setting, where the uniqueness of each child and family is celebrated. Children learn to have positive attitudes to others through the attitudes presented to them by the people who are significant in their lives.

Children's knowledge about people and communities begins at home within their unique family and is likely to differ significantly from one child to another – for some there may be lots of interaction outside the immediate home, while for others there may be few such opportunities. Involving and including parents is essential in helping practitioners to build on children's individual experiences, and create a 'community spirit' within the setting itself.

Involving parents in projects can foster children's awareness about others. The example quoted in Chapter 2 for Mother's Day in the reception class, not only involves the parents, but also children's sense of their own family history. When shared with the other children it provided a great opportunity for discussions about similarities and differences between families.

Asking parents to bring in photographs of themselves, as well as other relatives such as grandparents, and things that are important to the children at home, can result in wonderful projects, helping children to understand about the past and present, and the wider world, too. Parents can be asked to share rhymes and songs they like to sing at home with their children, or perhaps bring in CDs of music they play at home, broadening children's awareness of culture beyond their own immediate experience.

The local neighbourhood

Outings in the local neighbourhood can make a big impact on children's knowledge and understanding of the wider community – even simple trips such as taking a couple of children to the local shops to buy fruit for snack or ingredients for cooking can open up a range of possible discussions about the people they meet and what they see. Other visits out – such as to a local monument, church, mosque, temple or fire station – provide important learning experiences for children.

The wider community

Beyond the immediate experience of family and the local community, the best resources for children to help them understand about the wider human world beyond their immediate experience are information books and stories where the cultural setting is clearly different from their own. There are some wonderful ones available to us in the UK. If you are not familiar with them, the local library will help. In fact outings to the library, or visits from a mobile library can be a fantastic source of information for practitioners as well as the children.

Persona Dolls are mentioned in Development Matters (2012), in the section on 'Understanding the World: People and Communities', as a way to 'help children to learn positive attitudes and challenge negative attitudes and stereotypes'. They have been used in many settings around the UK very effectively as a way of helping children to develop positive attitudes to others, to challenge unfairness, and their own and others' negative attitudes. For more information see Chapter 4.

The World

This aspect of Understanding the World covers what we traditionally call 'science' in school. This includes observing and interacting with the natural world (plants and living things), and exploring the properties of materials. It involves children experiencing physical change, such as what happens when ingredients get mixed together when cooking or making dough, or when water is added to dry sand. It also covers 'geography' (a sense of place), as children find out about their immediate physical environment.

The Early Learning Goal, the expectation for the end of the reception year, states that:

> *Children know about similarities and differences in relation to places, objects, materials and living things. They talk about the features of their own immediate environment and how environments might vary from one another. They make observations of animals and plants and explain why some things occur, and talk about changes.* (EYFS, 2012)

Out of doors

The array of possible experiences that should be on offer is too great to list in detail here, but the outdoor environment provides the best opportunities and the best provision is when children can flow freely between the indoor and outdoor area. Children can experience what Garrick (2006) calls 'garden spaces' and 'wilder places'. If nothing else is available, a few deep planters for children to grow vegetables and flowers can suffice for the garden space, and a few rotting logs and pots of soil in a damp spot can suffice for the wilder places, so long as regular outings are also arranged.

I firmly believe that children need to spend *more* time out of doors in a rich, stimulating environment than they do inside. Children (and practitioners!) need all-weather clothing so that they can be out in all seasons and experience the weather first hand, creating experiments such as: how can we catch the rain? Which is the biggest puddle? Can we find a way to move the puddle? What happens to it when the sun comes out? They need opportunities to hunt for minibeasts, with practitioners on hand to prompt a discussion about what the children are finding, asking open-ended questions such as 'I wonder what/how/why?'

Encourage the children to develop skills in: observing, identifying, exploring, investigating, describing, thinking, wondering, asking questions and remembering.

Investigating

This aspect of Understanding the World lends itself to setting up investigations with children, following their interests and developing their thinking by encouraging their curiosity. But we need to be on hand to help. Marion Dowling talks about how practitioners *can* provide the inspiration for children, but do we do this enough?

> As co-players, adults may provoke the children's thinking through offering a new experience, pump prime and contribute to children's thoughts; they judge when it is appropriate to join in activities and sometimes offer snippets of inspiration and additional resources which refresh and re-invigorate children's views and ideas. (Dowling, 2008: 10)

Evangelou *et al.* (2009: 51) make the point that we do not do enough to 'convey to children the importance of not just "what happens" or "how it happens" but "why it happens"'. We need to be encouraging the *children* to ask the 'why' questions. The research the authors quote shows that children ask 'why' questions frequently at home, but not very often when they are in a setting or at school.

A Forest School outing

Many early years settings extend children's real first-hand experiences of the natural world through getting involved in the Forest School movement. The potential for learning for children of 3, 4 and more, across the full seven areas in the EYFS is huge.

Randolph Beresford Early Childhood Centre ensures that all the 3 and 4 year olds access their Forest School provision over the course of the year. A small group of children are involved one

Figure 9.2 Running in the long grass

day a week over a six-week period. The initial sessions involve training games about safety around the campfire and kettle, and getting dressed in their waterproof gear, as well as talking about what they might do in the woods. Then the trips out begin: to a local woodland area about a 20-minute walk away.

On this visit it was a very wet day. The children were given the option to go into the wood, under the trees or stay out in the open. They decided that under the trees was best. The children helped to put up a tarpaulin and pushed the logs into place for the camp. They found twigs for the fire, safety precautions were discussed, safety games played and the fire lit. The children helped to fill the storm kettle for their hot chocolate and watched it come to the boil.

After lunch they explored the wood, finding trees to climb (see Fig 6.3 in Chapter 6). Then Amari noticed a ladybird, telling the others excitedly about it. 'Look! A ladybird!' The ladybird is on the top of a hollow plant stalk and begins moving inside the hollow. 'Look,' said Amari, 'It's going down into the house. It's going to the bottom. It's got some food in there – oh it's stopped moving.' Elaine, the practitioner, and Amari discussed

Figure 9.3 Pushing logs into place for the camp

Figure 9.4 Getting ready to fill the storm kettle

Figure 9.5   Discussing the ladybird.

why it stopped moving – possibly it was asleep? Elaine asked how they might wake it. Amari: 'I think his Mummy might wake him up.' Elaine: 'What would she say?' Amari: 'Wake up please!'

Technology

The third aspect of this area of learning and development is Technology – not just computers, but ICT in its broadest sense. The Early Learning Goal is as follows:

> *Children recognise that a range of technology is used in places such as homes and schools. They select and use technology for particular purposes.* (EYFS, 2012)

Young children are very familiar with a range of technology in their daily lives, especially mobile phones, games consoles, televisions, DVD players and CD players, cameras and computers, laptops and iPads. They are interested in and excited about using these if they are available to them at a very early age. They are most likely to have had access to toys and books with electronic functions from a very early age, but they are usually most interested in the technology the adults around them use. Incorporating mobile phones and ordinary telephones is an important resource in the role-play area, for all children.

Many settings provide children in the nursery setting or reception class with child-friendly stills and video cameras so that they can record what interests them and their own work. Teaching them to download the photographs themselves is a valuable experience, and even sending email messages to their parents with the photographs attached, so long as this is in line with setting or school policy.

We need to be aware of the danger that children can become hooked on playing computer games, spending long periods sitting at a screen, often alone. We need to ensure that the game or program enables two to play and that children use the computer together (usually pairs is best). The programs should be educationally useful and should include open-ended programs such as those for drawing or painting.

Top tips for effective practice

- **Use books and stories** to support children's learning. Stories that accurately and positively depict people in cultural settings other than Britain are important resources.
- **Go on well-organised outings** in the local area and further afield, asking parents to come along. Make sure the safety rules for outings in your setting are adhered to.
- **Ensure all children and their families** feel they are important members of your group, by being inclusive.
- **Provide plenty of opportunities** to explore the world out of doors.
- **Make books**, using photographs taken by you and the children, about special events and celebrations, about activities, such as developing the garden area, and about their explorations and investigations.

Point for reflection

Do the resources in your setting reflect diversity? Think about your books: do they reflect and celebrate diversity and inclusion? Check for: ethnic diversity of the main characters, children with disabilities, boys in caring roles and girls in active roles. Think about posters and displays on the walls, home corner provision, games and puzzles: do they reflect diversity, too?

For a useful article about using technology in the early years go to: http://www.datec.org.uk/guidance/DATEC7.pdf

For more information about Forest Schools in the UK go to: http://www.forestschools.com/

10 Expressive Arts and Design

The EYFS describes the final specific area of learning and development, Expressive Arts and Design, in this way:

> *Expressive arts and design involves enabling children to explore and play with a wide range of media and materials, as well as providing opportunities and encouragement for sharing their thoughts, ideas and feelings through a variety of activities in art, music, movement, dance, role-play, and design and technology.* (EYFS, 2012: 1.6)

Expressive Arts and Design does not just cover what we label as 'art' (painting, drawing and sculpture) but *the arts*, some aspects of which are listed in the description. As Tina Bruce says:

> We are all so different in our modes of taking creative ideas to fruition. Some like to dance their ideas, some to make them into musical expressions. Some form scientific ideas or mathematical patterns, whilst others write poems and stories, make drawings, paintings, collages and sculptures and pottery. (Bruce, 2011: 92)

Expressive Arts and Design links closely with all areas of learning and development, prime and specific, and the Characteristics of Effective Learning describe how children develop their creative ideas.

Expressive Arts and Design in the EYFS is divided into two aspects:

1. Exploring and Using Media and Materials
2. Being Imaginative.

As we see from both the description of this area in the EYFS and the titles of the aspects, it is all about exploration and creative expression. The first aspect looks more at exploring the breadth of 'creative development', with an emphasis on *experimenting* and *doing*. The second focuses more on the imaginative/expressive side, how children *represent their creative ideas*. Drawing around templates or colouring in pictures has no place in the EYFS, neither has the 'assembly line' approach where each child is expected to produce the same product. These types of activities do not help children to develop creative expression or meaningful skills, and are more likely to knock their confidence in their own abilities and result in a 'can't do' attitude.

'Creativity does not come from nowhere. It feeds off our experiences. It depends on them for creative ideas to develop' (Bruce 2011: 92). For babies and toddlers the creative process is very much an exploratory one, but creative exploration also continues throughout life as we ask questions when encountering something new, such as: *What is this material like? What can I do with it?* As babies and toddlers develop, imagination kicks in and young children begin to express themselves in creative ways while exploring their own capabilities and the world around. When we provide rich and varied experiences, and show how much we value children's creative expressions, children will come to value and appreciate their own creative expression.

Exploring and Using Media and Materials

The Early Learning Goal for the end of the reception year for this aspect of Expressive Arts and Design is:

> *Children sing songs, make music and dance, and experiment with ways of changing them. They safely use and explore a variety of materials, tools and techniques, experimenting with colour, design, texture, form and function.* (EYFS, 2012)

Exploration through play and child-initiated activity must always come first, but children also need to learn some techniques and how to use appropriate tools once they have had plenty of exploratory experiences.

Exploring materials and media in two dimensions

Drawing and painting begin with exploring mark making. Babies begin to explore the patterns visually and then through their own movements. As they grow and develop we need to provide a wide variety of opportunities for children to mark make, so that they can use as much movement as they need to. Possibilities include water on a dry surface, cornflour gloop, jelly and gels, wet sand, shaving foams and finger painting. Hands and fingers are the best tools, introducing other tools such as crayons, pencils, pens and brushes only when they have had plenty of experiences using their hands.

Emma, aged 2 yrs 4 mths, has had many experiences at home and at nursery to make marks and play at drawing. She was very motivated and decisive when she made these marks. She had been given a new set of felt tips and went through each one in turn making deliberate and separate scribble patterns. Each time, she took the lid off the pen and placed it back on when she had finished. Once she had gone through the pack she used some colours again and, at the end, made the enclosed shape on the bottom right-hand corner of Fig 10.1. She did not talk about what she had done when she had finished as this was an exploration; she did not ascribe meaning to her marks. However, during the process she quietly talked to herself: 'Now yellow one, now blue one, green one', and so on. She was clearly enjoying this careful exploration, looking satisfied when she had finished, then moved off to something else.

A few weeks later Emma's mark making is sometimes representational drawings (Fig 10.2).

Figure 10.1 Emma's mark making

Figure 10.2 Emma's drawing of herself

Exploring materials and media in three dimensions

Open-ended materials such as clay and wooden blocks for building give children the best opportunities for exploring in three dimensions, leading them to explore their properties, and gradually understand how the materials work and the myriad of possibilities that can be tried out with them.

For toddlers, Heuristic Play, developed by Elinor Goldschmied, is an invaluable experience for calm and quiet exploration. It involves providing a wide range of different natural materials, such as fir cones, cardboard tubes, short ribbon and chains, ping pong balls, wooden rings and shells, in collections for exploring. Heuristic means discovery and, in this discovery play, toddlers discover the properties of the materials through using all their senses, by using a range of movements, and follow their own trains of thought and action. It is a quiet and contemplative time, where the practitioners remain quiet and attentive without interfering.

A creative workshop area for children, with a similar wide range of natural materials as well as recyclable materials – bottle tops, plastic cartons, cardboard boxes, etc. – should be provided for older children (2–5 yrs and older) to explore, place and arrange, and also to join together in their own ways. With plenty of experience children will begin to represent their ideas, but much exploration needs to take place first. A wide range of possible materials for joining should also be provided, such as sticky tape, string and ribbon – not just glue. Many settings also provide children with opportunities to engage in woodwork (see Fig 10.3).

Music, movement and dance

When babies hear music we usually see them bounce and rock to the rhythm delightedly. This continues through childhood, with children able to make increasingly refined movements and dance, so long as it is encouraged by adults around and provision is made for it.

As well as regularly singing, simple percussion instruments provide children with important experiences to make a range of

Figure 10.3   Woodwork can provide a great opportunity to explore materials and be creative

rhythms using a range of movements. Eventually they will be able to copy a beat, repeat a beat and make up a pattern of beats for themselves. Listening to a wide range of different music, with different tempo, pitch and instruments, as well as music from different cultural heritages, will give them a valuable opportunity to experience music they may not find in their daily lives outside the setting, to dance, move to or just to listen to. It is important that this is not as background music but is there for a purpose when they can listen more attentively.

The adult role in supporting creative exploration

The first and most important aspect of the adult role in supporting children's creative development is to provide not just a variety of opportunities and experiences for open-ended exploration, but also encouragement so that children will explore for pleasure and experiment creatively – and, of course, safely! When they are ready children need to be taught specific skills and techniques to enhance their experiences, and to use tools appropriately and safely. Observing them helps to decide when might be the right moment, to prevent a child becoming frustrated.

Being Imaginative

It is interesting that the final aspect of all the areas of learning is called 'being imaginative', which almost brings us back full circle to a key aspect of the Characteristics of Effective Learning (see Chapter 1). Being imaginative is not only an important part of how we learn, but also how we function day to day, moment by moment, using our imaginations and thinking ahead, planning what we intend to do next. However, in the context of Expressive Arts and Design, 'being imaginative' is more specific, relating to how children use their imagination in their creative experiences.

The Early Learning Goal, for children at the end of reception is:

> *Children use what they have learnt about media and materials in original ways, thinking about users and purposes. They represent their own ideas, thoughts and feelings through design and technology, art, music, dance, role play and stories.* (EYFS, 2012)

It is not usually until children are 3 years old or so, once they have had lots of experience of exploration, that they usually begin to ascribe meaning to their marks or three-dimensional explorations, or view anything they do as representational. We need to take care that we do not impose on the children our views or ideas of what things should look like.

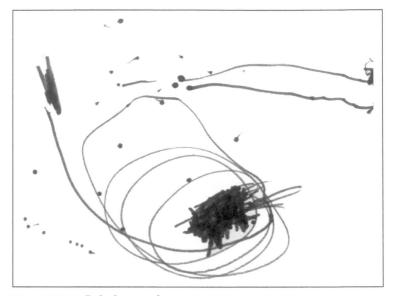

Figure 10.4 Daisy's sea eels

Figure 10.4 shows a drawing by Daisy, aged 3 yrs 3 mths. Her mother said:

> *The drawings were on small paper because Daisy wanted to make postcards. This one is 'sea eels' (Daisy lives very near the sea and sea life is an important part of her life). The straight lines are the sea eels and the solid patch is drawn like that to show that the eels can't go in there. I think this comes from us discussing signs saying 'no admittance' that she was interested in when we were on the ferry recently.*

Role play

This is the first time that role play is mentioned in an Early Learning Goal, but we know it is so vital to children's learning, as discussed in most of the chapters in this book. Role play, 'pretend play' and 'fantasy play' are key ways in which children express their imaginations as they explore relationships, ideas and stories, as well as their own developing skills. This kind of play does not begin usually until about 18 months old or so, as toddlers imitate what they see others do. Tina Bruce and her colleagues talk about

> the development of play through pretend, imagination, symbols and a well-coordinated body (18 mths/2 yrs to 5, 6, 7 years). As play develops, children become increasingly able to engage in a world of pretend. They can imagine things beyond the literal and real imitation of things. They can move from the present into the past and the future and as they do so they transform things. (Bruce *et al.*, 2010: 357)

Our role as practitioners and parents is to be attentive to what the children are showing interest in, provide the provocations for children to be imaginative in their child-initiated activities, such as reading imaginative and playful stories, as well as helping them let their imaginations flow and giving them time to think: 'Remember that the world out of doors lends itself to inspiration from the weather and the sights, sounds and textures of the environment' (Hutchin, 2012).

Top tips for effective practice

- **Provide a learning environment** rich in potential for all aspects of creative and artistic expression, role play, music, dance and art in two and three dimensions. Allow plenty of time and space, especially making use of the outdoor environment.
- **Find out more about** Heuristic Play for toddlers (for example, on YouTube or at http://coreexperiences.wikia. com/wiki/Treasure_Basket_and_Heuristic_Play

- **Provide:**
  - a well-resourced creative workshop area
  - musical instruments for babies and young children to explore and try out
  - imaginative and playful songs and stories
  - CDs of music from different cultures to listen and move to.

Point for reflection

For 2–5 year olds: if you already have a creative workshop area, are the resources and tools displayed so that children can help themselves and see the potential? Can children find what they need and help themselves? And, when they are ready, are they taught the skills to use the tools? Is there a variety of resources such as boxes of all shapes and sizes, lolly sticks, matchsticks, cardboard tubes, bottle tops, paper, ribbon, fabric, etc.? How much variety is there in resources for joining? How often is an adult in the area to support children in their explorations and creative ideas? If your setting does not have a creative workshop area, arrange to set one up.

11 Ensuring Children's Progress Through Assessment and Planning

In this chapter we discuss the assessment processes necessary for effective practice in the early years, including the day-to-day assessments made as you observe, work with and support the children, and summative assessments that are needed at various points in time. There are two statutory summative assessments: one for children aged between 2 and 3 (the Progress Check at Age Two) and the Early Years Foundation Stage Profile (EYFSP) carried out by reception teachers at the very end of the EYFS. As this book is primarily for those working in nursery settings, we look in detail only at the Progress Check here.

Observation and effective practice

Planning is effective only if it is based on what we are finding out about how and what children are learning. Observing is a key aspect of the practitioner role – so important that it is a requirement in the Statutory Framework:

> *Ongoing assessment (also known as formative assessment) is an integral part of the learning and development process. It involves practitioners observing children to understand their level of achievement, interests and learning styles, and to then shape learning experiences for each child reflecting those observations. In their interactions with children, practitioners should respond to their own day-to-day observations about children's progress, and observations that parents and carers share.* (EYFS, 2012: 2.1)

The EYFS, particularly Development Matters (Early Education, 2012), provides a broad guide as to what needs to be planned in general terms, ensuring 'coverage' of all seven areas of learning, and considering the three Characteristics of Effective Learning, but to meet the children's needs, our observations and knowledge of the children we are responsible for are essential. It is also a really enjoyable aspect of the practitioner role, teasing out what to offer next on the basis of what the children are doing and thinking.

Formative assessment: the observation, assessment and planning cycle

Formative assessment is assessment that is used to *inform* planning, or as the Statutory Framework puts it, observing children to shape appropriate learning experiences for them. The diagram in Fig 11.1 helps to explain how this works. We need to

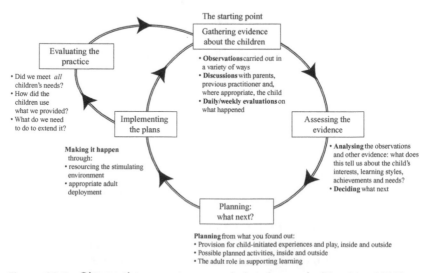

Figure 11.1 Observation, assessment and planning cycle (Hutchin, 2007)

start planning by 'gathering evidence', finding out about the children from observing them in action and discussing with parents what they are doing at home. The evidence is then analysed, to make an assessment, asking: what does this observation tell me about the child's learning and development? Then comes the planning stage: what shall we offer next? The plans are implemented and the cycle starts again. Observing also has another purpose, which is to help us evaluate the provision we made. How did the children respond? Did it meet their needs and interests?

What to observe

Even though the revised EYFS Statutory Framework makes observing a requirement, it also echoes a concern raised by many practitioners: that they are spending too much time writing up observations.

> *Assessment should not entail prolonged breaks from interaction with children nor require excessive paperwork. Paperwork should be limited to that which is absolutely necessary to promote children's successful learning and development.* (EYFS, 2012: 2.2)

So how should practitioners observe, and how should their observations be recorded? There are various methods for observing and recording observations, the most common of which currently are short snippets recorded on sticky notes or self-adhesive labels, which are then added to the child's 'profile' or 'learning journal'. Photographs are a particularly useful type of observation, but they also need to be analysed as shown in Fig 11.1 and described below.

My own view is that the most useful type of observation is the longer observation where the practitioner stands back to observe. This is so useful for capturing the children at play and child-initiated learning, where you will see not only the child applying what they know and can do, but also the approach they take and their particular interests. In these observations you are more likely to pick up things you did not know. It involves standing back to watch and listen for a few minutes only, three or four minutes or so, taking photographs as well as making a few notes – especially, when possible, writing down what the child said or communicated non-verbally.

Organising the observations

These 'standing back' observations do not have to be made on each child very often, so long as they are of children busy in a rich learning environment that engages them and provokes their involvement. But it is important to make sure that every child is observed in this way. Many settings organise this by taking each child in turn to be the 'focus child' for a week and, during that time, make sure a longer observation has been made. In Randolph Beresford Children's Centre, it works like this:

> We take each child in rotation as a 'focus child' for a week (2 focus children per week). Each child becomes the focus child once per term. The week before the focus week for the child we ask parents about what their child is doing and is showing interest in at home.

Making the assessment: analysing the observation

An observation is of no use unless it is analysed, to draw out what the observation is showing about what and how the child is learning. Every observation of play and child-initiated learning will provide information about *more* than one area of learning and development, and often information about learning in three or four areas can be seen. The box gives an example of the observation, assessment and planning cycle in action.

William: 1 yr 8 mths

Built up coloured blocks and knocked them down, repeating this many times. Separated out the yellow blocks and transported them to where a shape-matching game was set out. Continued to build up the yellow blocks, placing some of the yellow flat shapes from the game on top of the blocks. Then started to match yellow shapes on to some of the boards from the game, matching by colour, yellow on yellow, rather than by shape. Made vocal sounds, including words: 'aah, look, ooh, mine, aah'. Spoke to other children who joined in, making vocal sounds and excited facial expressions. Moved on to join other children playing with dry pasta, saucepans and a cooker. Filled up a pan, gave out pasta to the others, vocalising as he did so. Put pan of pasta on the cooker and blew on it to cool it.

Assessment

What learning was in evidence?

Prime areas
PSED: keen and confident to interact with others. **C and L:** using some single words, lots of vocal sounds strung together as in conversation, and non-verbal communication. Enthusiastic to communicate. **Physical:** carefully built up blocks using skill to balance both large blocks and small shapes.

Specific areas
Mathematics: showing interest in matching by colour, aware of shapes that will balance on top of one another; **UW:** developing awareness of properties of a range of materials and exploring what he can do with them; **EAD:** involved in imaginative play – sharing out food, pretending to blow to cool food.

How was he learning?

Playing and exploring a range of materials; willing to try things out; active learning: very absorbed in what he was doing, at same time as socialising with others.

Possibilities for planning

Introduce William to the wide range of different types of blocks we have inside and outside; involve him in cooking activities – e.g. really cooking pasta, making soup – and sharing out food.

And on to planning...

From the analysis or assessment, it usually becomes quite clear what opportunities and possibilities might be appropriate to present to the child next, and unless this is recorded in some way, it is easy to forget it. These planning points need to be taken to the planning meeting or to the vital evaluation meeting at the end of each day.

Creating a record for each child

In most settings you will find individual folders or booklets for each child, stored accessibly so that child, parent and practitioners have access to them. They are usually full of the observations, photographs and samples (such as mark making, drawing and early writing) the child has made. It is best not to divide them into separate sections for each area of learning, as any observation will show more than one area of learning, as in the example above, and this will only increase the paperwork.

Keeping the records accessible is a great way to involve not only the children but parents as well. It will encourage parents to tell you what their child is doing at home. Figure 11.2 shows Billy (3 yrs 1 mth) in a daycare setting, looking at his 'profile folder' with his mother. His mother is delighted by what she sees.

Figure 11.2 Billy and his mother look through his profile folder together

In Fig 11.3 two children are looking at their profile with their key person. The profile folders are favourite books for the children, to be looked at and read, often many times a day.

Evaluating the day and the week

A short, daily evaluation meeting, at the end of each day, is an invaluable opportunity to consider what has happened during the session and adjust planning for the following day. If this is not

Figure 11.3

possible – for example, if staff are on shifts – it is important for the room leader to have a brief chat with staff about how they feel the day went and what they observed, so that she/he can adjust the planning for the next day.

At the Stay and Play provision in Old Oak Children's Centre, the team make time for an evaluation meeting at the end of every session, where they share what they observed. As this is a 'drop in', different children and parents may attend each day. The team evaluate what went well, what needs more thought, setting out differently, extending, or more practitioner time with the children and parents.

Not only do we plan carefully on the basis of our evaluation – just as you would for any group of children – we develop things as we go along in the session, based on the children's interests.

Although there is a core of parents who come regularly, we never know exactly who is coming, so we need to be very responsive during the session, for example getting different things out to address children's interests.

In Randolph Beresford Children's Centre, where children stay all day, daily evaluations take place in every room. The Under Threes Team Leader, Lizzie, explained:

We base our weekly planning on what has been happening the previous week, adding in plans for the previous week's focus children. The daily evaluation meetings are really important for us – we all sit down and evaluate the day together. As a result of these we change our plans for the next day. The most important thing is that we respond to the children!

From formative to summative assessment

Summative assessment is just what it sounds like – a summary of the child's learning, summarising the observations, conversations with parents, child and anyone else involved. When these are made regularly they help us to see the progress that a child is making.

It is up to the setting to decide how best to do this and there is no advice or guidance relating to it in the EYFS, but it is something that Ofsted inspectors, who inspect the quality of all early years settings, will look for. In the 'Evaluation schedule for inspections of registered early years provision', the guidance for inspectors July 2012, inspectors are asked to look for 'evidence of assessment that includes the progress of different groups of children'. This includes

> assessment on entry, including parental contributions … ongoing (formative) assessments, including any parental contributions … evidence of planning for children's next stages of learning based on staff assessment and a secure knowledge of the characteristics of learning and children's development. (Ofsted, 2012a: 7)

Making a summary

Over a period of time there will be a collection of 'evidence' of learning, from discussions with parents, photographs of significant things you see the child do and occasional longer observations, such as the one of William in this chapter. In Randolph Beresford Children's Centre the staff summarise each child's learning and development every three months, at the time when the child becomes the 'focus child' for the week. The key person summarises what they know, discusses this with parents and together they devise some possibilities for planning for the child, which they begin to implement the following week. Some plans, of course, are longer term, particularly those relating to the prime areas of learning. As they work with the children, the staff observe the child's responses to what has been planned and the outcomes and the cycle of planning and support continues.

In Fig 11.4 you will see the format they use to record the summary. Staff find the 'Adult Attention' box, which was recently added to the format, very helpful. This is where they specify how the key person will support the child.

The statutory summative assessments

The EYFS has two statutory assessments that practitioners must undertake. We will begin with a brief explanation of the final assessment at the end of the EYFS and then explain in more detail the 'Progress Check at Age Two'.

The Early Years Foundation Stage Profile

The EYFS Profile is the statutory assessment at the very end of the EYFS, at the end of the reception year. Each child is assessed in relation to the 17 Early Learning Goals (ELGs). The assessment is based on the ongoing records collected over time:

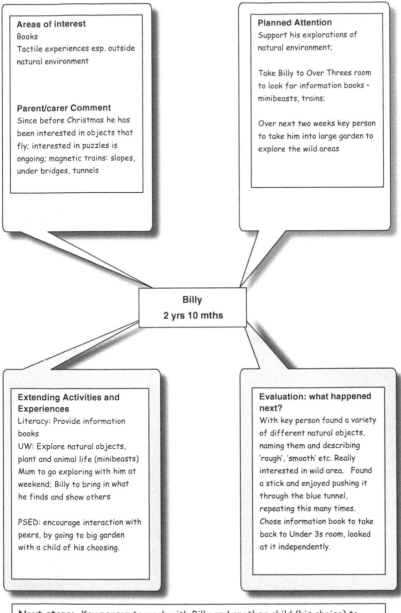

Areas of interest
Books
Tactile experiences esp. outside
natural environment

Parent/carer Comment
Since before Christmas he has
been interested in objects that
fly; interested in puzzles is
ongoing; magnetic trains: slopes,
under bridges, tunnels

Planned Attention
Support his explorations of
natural environment;

Take Billy to Over Threes room
to look for information books –
minibeasts, trains;

Over next two weeks key person
to take him into large garden to
explore the wild areas

Billy
2 yrs 10 mths

Extending Activities and
Experiences
Literacy: Provide information
books
UW: Explore natural objects,
plant and animal life (minibeasts)
Mum to go exploring with him at
weekend; Billy to bring in what
he finds and show others

PSED: encourage interaction with
peers, by going to big garden
with a child of his choosing.

Evaluation: what happened
next?
With key person found a variety
of different natural objects,
naming them and describing
'rough', 'smooth' etc. Really
interested in wild area. Found
a stick and enjoyed pushing it
through the blue tunnel,
repeating this many times.
Chose information book to take
back to Under 3s room, looked
at it independently.

Next steps: Key person to work with Billy and another child (his choice) to
continue supporting him in developing interaction with other children.

Figure 11.4 Randolph Beresford termly review format

> *The Profile must reflect ongoing observation; all relevant records held by the setting; discussions with parents and carers, and any other adults whom the teacher, parent or carer judges can offer a useful contribution.* (EYFS, 2012: 2.7)

The final assessments, made in June each year, are 'best fit' judgements, taking each ELG and deciding whether the child has met it and is therefore at 'the expected level', has exceeded this level ('exceeding'), or not yet met it ('emerging'). In addition to judging the child against the 17 ELGs there is a requirement to provide information with regard to the Characteristics of Effective Learning to assist with planning in Year 1:

> *Year 1 teachers must be given a copy of the Profile report together with a short commentary on each child's skills and abilities in relation to the three key Characteristics of Effective Learning.* (EYFS, 2012: 2.8)

The Progress Check at Age Two

The revised EYFS introduced a new statutory assessment to be carried out by practitioners, including childminders, working with children aged between 2 and 3 yrs.

> *When a child is aged between two and three, practitioners must review their progress, and provide parents and/or carers with a short written summary of their child's development in the prime areas.* (EYFS, 2012: 2.3)

Many practitioners, providers and experts were surprised by this new statutory assessment as most children do not attend any setting until they are 3 and statutory education starts in the term after children are aged 5. However, the rationale for it is to flag up if a child is in need of additional support to ensure this is provided at the earliest opportunity.

> *This progress check must identify the child's strengths, and any areas where the child's progress is less than expected. If there are significant emerging concerns, or an identified special educational need or disability, practitioners should develop a targeted plan to support the child's future learning and development involving other professionals (for example, the provider's Special Educational Needs Co-ordinator) as appropriate.* (EYFS, 2012: 2.3)

Unusually for a statutory assessment, there is no specific format to be used and no particular time at which this summary should be made. Many settings already make regular summaries of every child's learning from the beginning of their time in the setting, as described in the previous section, and the setting's own preferred format could be used so long as the required information is included: 'Beyond the prime areas, it is for practitioners to decide what the written summary should include' (EYFS, 2012: 2.4).

There is a clear aspiration in the Statutory Framework that the Progress Check, created on the basis of the ongoing accumulated observations and assessments of the child, will be used to inform Health Visitors as they carry out the Two Year Health Review.

> *It should be provided in time to inform the Healthy Child Programme health and development review at age two whenever possible (when health visitors gather information on a child's health and development, allowing them to identify any developmental delay and any particular support from which they think the child/family might benefit).* (EYFS, 2012: 2.5)

However, as the Progress Check only goes to parents/carers, this is entirely up to the parent. The Parent's Guide to the EYFS states only that:

> *You might find it useful to share the information from the check with other professionals such as health visitors (who can use it as part of the health and development review).* (Parents Guide to the EYFS, 2012: 7)

At the time of writing a plan is in place to bring together, by 2015, the Health Review made by Health Visitors with the Progress Check into one 'integrated' check. In the meantime it is important for managers and practitioners to encourage parents to share the Progress Check with their Health Visitor.

The 'Healthy Child' health and development review

In the Two Year Health Review carried out by Health Visitors, the child's gross motor development, vision and fine motor development, hearing and speech development, social behaviour and play are generally checked. This check is very different from the summary written by the practitioner, which is based on accumulated knowledge of the child. It is usually carried out in a health clinic, based on assessments made during the appointment, as the child plays with the toys provided or is asked to carry out an age-appropriate activity. The assessment is also based on discussions with the parent who is present at the time. A check is made on walking, climbing (usually the Health Visitor will check if the child can climb on and off a chair easily), and height, weight and head circumference. Health Visitors find Mary Sheridan's well-known and well-respected, *Birth to Five* guidance a useful reference resource (Sheridan, 2008), as well as the Healthy Child Programme Guidance (2009).

The Health Check provides a useful time for discussion with parents about health and safety, diet and nutrition, and any concerns they may have about their child – for example, their child's social behaviour, play or language development. If the Health Visitor picks up a concern about the child's development, a referral will be made – for example, for a hearing test and speech and language therapy support, or another appropriate specialist service.

Speaking to a Health Visitor recently, she felt very positive about practitioners carrying out a different kind of 'check' on the child, as this would complement what Health Visitors do, providing a different perspective because the practitioner will know the child well and can assess them over time. The result is likely to be much more comprehensive if the two checks came together in this way.

Carrying out the Progress Check at Age Two

The short 'Know How Guide' on carrying out the Progress Check at Age Two, produced by the National Children's Bureau (2012), is the only government-endorsed guidance. One of the most useful aspects of this guidance is the process it promotes for carrying out the check:

- Review and reflect upon the child
- Draft some comments or make initial assessment judgements
- Discuss the child's progress with parents or carers, taking their views into account
- Discuss any concerns about the child with the leader/ manager of the setting...
- Finalise the progress check.

(NCB, 2012: 13)

A young child may spend many hours in the setting, but their parents always know them best, so sharing what is proposed in a draft assessment before the check is finalised is the most important part of the process. It is also essential that nothing written in the check comes as a surprise to the parents. A useful comment from a parent is recorded in the guidance:

> If I was given a report or document written about my son, I would like the report to show that the person who has written it really knows him. Of course I know exactly what he can do when he is at home, because I am watching him and listening to him every day, but I would want to know what he shows when he isn't with me, on the days when he is at nursery. (NCB, 2012: 11)

At the Old Oak Children's Centre, staff compile the Progress Check for children in the crèches and those who regularly attend the Stay and Play:

> *Completing the Progress Check with the parent is a very positive experience as the parents can add in so much about the children when they are not here. It is really good to sit down together and*

talk. Parents are so pleased that we know their children well. We make the assessment judgements together, using Development Matters and this helps parents understand the kind of things we look for. As one mother told me: 'This is really useful. As a parent I just don't have time to stand back and reflect on my child and what he is learning and what his interests are.'

Using Development Matters

There is no one way of making the summary assessment, but some kind of criteria against which to make the assessment is necessary, to avoid the possibility that everyone completing the check coming up with a different view about 'where the child's progress is less than expected' (EYFS, 2012: 2.3).

The most obvious answer is to use the Development Matters age bands, to make a best-fit judgement on the band as a whole. Start with the 22–36-month band: does the child fit securely within this age band? If not, is she/he ahead or not yet at this stage? Even though it is guidance, and therefore not a requirement, Development Matters is also the document that Ofsted inspectors are expected to use in looking at whether a setting is helping children make progress or not.

Although there is no particular format to use, some samples are provided in the guidance. The following two Progress Checks, carried out by the key person for the two children concerned, who is also the Under Threes Team Leader, used Example 2 in the Guidance (produced by Early Learning Consultancy) as a model for the version she used.

I found this format useful because it gives you freedom to put in a comment on each of the prime areas as a whole so that you can highlight specific aspects which are important about the child, rather than feeling you have to write the same length of comment against each aspect of the area. To make the summative judgment I looked through the child's profile, where we collect all the observations, parents' comments etc., and then looked

Two year Old Progress Check

Name Ibrahim   Date 5th October 2012   Age 2 Years 10 Months

How this child is learning	Personal, Social and Emotional Development
Playing and exploring:	*Self confidence and self-awareness; Making relationships; Managing feelings and behaviour.*
Active Learning:	
Creating and thinking critically	Ibrahim has formed good relationships with certain staff and children in the setting. He will initiate 'peek-a-boo' games and laugh and smile with selected adults and peers. Ibrahim has strong interests, and therefore usually
Ibrahim often revisits activities and resources which excite and interest him. He is a 'collector' and a 'transporter', and therefore when he finds objects that he wants to collect and transport – cars, shells, stones, collage materials, hair bands, animals – he will do so for the majority of the session. Ibrahim's collections often interest other children, as he will also line up and move around the various objects that he has found. When Ibrahim is highly motivated by something he shows good persistence and concentration.	tends to play alongside other children who share his interests – such as the cars, trains and small world animals. At times Ibrahim finds it difficult to share, and he will resort to pushing and snatching in order to obtain (or retain) the particular toy that he wants. At times like this, Ibrahim needs to be reminded to use words instead of actions to achieve his desired outcome. Ibrahim has now learnt to say "my turn" when he wants to play with something, and is encouraged to say "stop" along with the hand gesture when conflict arises.

Self-Confidence and self-awareness

0-11	8-20	16-26	22-36	30-50	40-60
		16-26			

Making relationships

0-11	8-20	16-26	22-36	30-50	40-60
		16-26			

Managing feelings and behaviour

0-11	8-20	16-26	22-36	30-50	40-60
		16-26			

Communication and Language	Physical Development
Listening and attention; Understanding; Speaking.	*Moving and handling; Health and self-care.*
Ibrahim increasingly understands what is happening around him and the words that are spoken. He has learnt some phrases which he uses regularly, such as "my turn" and will repeat single words that he hears spoken by an adult. Ibrahim's delayed speech and language have been a cause of concern, and because of this he was referred for speech and language therapy. Upon assessment it was determined that Ibrahim needed support in this area, which he is in the process of receiving. Ibrahim has taken part in language groups within the setting. During the block of 6 groups Ibrahim showed fantastic progress. He was able to follow all the instructions and join in with the song actions and some of the words – demonstrating good concentration throughout.	Ibrahim is able to use strong and purposeful movements, and shows confidence in terms of his gross motor skills. Ibrahim has shown a preference for exploring the climbing equipment in the garden, and has begun to attempt to jump off a low beam with the support of an adult. Ibrahim often spends time on the three wheeled bike, and will use both legs to propel himself around the garden. Ibrahim is also developing his fine motor skills, by accessing cooking activities when they are available, where he has learnt to safely cut using a knife. Ibrahim has so far shown no interest in using the toilet, and does not indicate when he is soiled or wet. As he still wears nappies, Ibrahim has limited opportunity to attempt to dress himself, however he is completely co-operative when having his nappy changed.

Listening and attention

0-11	8-20	16-26	22-36	30-50	40-60
		16-26			

Understanding

0-11	8-20	16-26	22-36	30-50	40-60
		16-26			

Moving and handling

0-11	8-20	16-26	22-36	30-50	40-60
			22-36		

Speaking

0-11	8-20	16-26	22-36	30-50	40-60
	8-20				

Health and self-care

0-11	8-20	16-26	22-36	30-50	40-60
		16-26			

Next Steps to support learning and development:
For Ibrahim to be interested in others play and start to join in.
For Ibrahim to begin to put two words together (e.g. "want ball" or "more juice").

Parent(s) signature and comment:	**Key Person Signature:**
I'm worried about his speech but I will continue to take him to therapy. I'm pleased he's stopped hitting and learnt to say no. He's now very patient with his brothers and sister when he wants something - like the computer. He's able to wait for his turn. He's also now sitting at the table for his food, before he was always coming and going. He's learnt all that here at nursery.	

Figure 11.5 Ibrahim's Progress Check at Age Two

Progress Check at Age Two

Name Kimarla   Date 5th October 2012   Age 2 Years 10 Months

How this child is learning	Personal, Social and Emotional Development
Playing and exploring; *Active Learning;* *Creating and thinking critically* Kimarla has a very positive approach to learning. As well as regularly revisiting activities and resources that she is interested in and familiar with, she is a child that is always willing to take part in new learning opportunities. Kimarla will initiate new sequences of play, and therefore acts as a role model for other children in the group by introducing new ideas. Kimarla uses her knowledge and experience from outside of the setting to initiate conversations, make connections, and link together ideas and thoughts.	*Self confidence and self-awareness; Making relationships; Managing feelings and behaviour.* Kimarla will regularly seek out familiar adults in the room who she has built trusting and positive relationships with. She is a very sociable child, and will initiate new conversations, as well as join existing ones. Kimarla knows the other children and shows empathy towards them, for example spontaneously getting a tissue when someone is crying. Kimarla is beginning to play co-operatively with her peers, but on the whole she tends to play alongside them. Kimarla usually responds well to boundaries. Occasionally she will become upset when she's frustrated, for example not being able to get a sleeve of her coat on. In times like this she needs a small amount of reassurance and a reminder that all she has to do is ask for help. Kimarla is able to quickly engage in play once she is happy again.

Self-Confidence and self-awareness

0-11	8-20	16-26	22-36	30-50	40-60
			22-36		

Making relationships

0-11	8-20	16-26	22-36	30-50	40-60
			22-36		

Managing feelings and behaviour

0-11	8-20	16-26	22-36	30-50	40-60
			22-36		

Communication and Language	Physical Development
Listening and attention; Understanding; Speaking. Kimarla is a confident communicator. She increasingly puts words together to form longer sentences and engage in prolonged conversations. At times Kimarla's speech sounds are difficult to understand, but she is able to use gestures and other words to make herself understood. Kimarla has shown a preference for singing, and during group times she will actively take part in choosing songs, completing the actions and singing along. Kimarla is interested in books, and demonstrates age appropriate concentration while listening to a story. Kimarla is confident and keen to join in with repeated refrains, and will enthusiastically answer questions about stories she is familiar with.	*Moving and handling; Health and self-care.* Kimarla will spend long periods of time outside in the garden, where she will use the space to confidently walk, run and skip. Kimarla regularly accesses the climbing equipment, and has developed her confidence and skill on the various levels of climbing equipment available to her. In the large nursery garden, Kimarla is able to independently use the big slide, and she will also spend time on the three wheeled bikes and scooters. Kimarla has also developed her fine motor skills, and is able to use scissors to snip paper, as well as mark making tools in a three fingered tripod grip Kimarla has now mastered using the toilet independently. She occasionally needs support in pulling up and fastening her trousers. Kimarla shows pride in herself when she has successfully used the toilet.

Listening and attention

0-11	8-20	16-26	22-36	30-50	40-60
			22-36		

Understanding

0-11	8-20	16-26	22-36	30-50	40-60
			22-36		

Speaking

0-11	8-20	16-26	22-36	30-50	40-60
			22-36		

Moving and handling

0-11	8-20	16-26	22-36	30-50	40-60
			22-36		

Health and self-care

0-11	8-20	16-26	22-36	30-50	40-60
			22-36		

Next Steps to support learning and development:
For Kimarla to be able to express feelings such as sad, happy, cross, scared or worried.
For Kimarla to build up her vocabulary to reflect the breadth of her experiences.

Parent(s) signature and comment:	Key Person Signature:
I think Kimarla's come a long way from when she started at nursery to now. Especially with her speech. It's still unclear but she's talking a whole lot more. I think maybe she was shy before.	

Figure 11.6 Kimarla's Progress Check at Age Two

at the Development Matters statements. The band entered onto the form was the one which fit best with the child's development and achievements to date, where s/he met most of the descriptions. The 'Characteristics of Learning' is a really positive addition to the form. It helped me bring out the uniqueness of the child, what is special about them and how they are learning.

Completing the Progress Check is adding something to our assessment processes which we were not doing before, although we make regular summaries through our 'focus child' reviews. The focus on the three prime areas in more depth is really useful, giving us a deeper look at the fundamentals. Organising the check between the age of two and three years means it is completed during the child's time with us, it isn't a transition record for the next setting, This means we are not passing the responsibility for any action resulting from the Check to someone else but we follow it up ourselves, together with the parents, and it helps us keep track of the outcomes.

Top tips for effective practice

- **Ensure your planning** is informed by your observations of children at play and in child-initiated activities.
- **Remember** that observations need to be analysed to make an assessment and be of use in planning.
- **Talk with parents** regularly and frequently about what their child is doing at home.
- **Summarise** every child's record from time to time.
- **Complete the Progress Check at Age Two** *with* the parent.

Point for reflection

Planning on the basis of your observation helps ensure that what is provided is tailored to the needs of the children. Refer back to Fig 11.1. How do practitioners in your setting make this happen? If you are in a setting with 2 year olds, how will you make sure that parents are fully involved in the Progress Check?

12 Using the EYFS to Evaluate Practice

It has been a pleasure to visit the inspiring settings used in the examples of practice and the observations of children in this book, watching the contented, engaged and well-cared-for children and the reflective practitioners enjoying their work with them, reflecting on what works best for each unique individual child. At the same time as continuing with their high-quality work these practitioners were also considering the implications of the newly revised EYFS Framework and what changes would be necessary for them to make while holding on to the good practice they had already established. Here are some of their views about the revised EYFS.

Under Threes Team Leader, Lizzie:

> *We are used to change in the early years. What I like best about the revised EYFS is the much greater emphasis on the characteristics of learning. This is a really useful addition. By prioritising this it confirms that what we do and what we provide for the children makes a big difference. I also like the increased emphasis on the prime areas which we have always known are so important but now these are acknowledged as the foundations of learning and development.*

Myrtle, Children's Centre teacher, agreed with the views expressed by Lizzie, but added:

> *The revised EYFS has provided a good opportunity to think about our own practice and what else we could be doing. In our centre our work is with parents as well as with the children. Compiling the children's Learning Journey booklets with the parents means we regularly make time to talk about their children's*

development and learning with them, but the Progress Check at Age Two has given us an opportunity to reflect together in a slightly different way, summarising where the child is in their learning and development and how they are learning too. Making the assessment judgements with the parent, using Development Matters together, has helped us share in more detail their knowledge of their child and our knowledge of child development.

Celebrating strengths and identifying areas for development

Ofsted is responsible for ensuring everyone working with young children implements the EYFS effectively for children within the EYFS age range. All schools and early years settings in England are inspected under the Ofsted inspection framework. Inspectors examine the quality of provision and how it is supporting children to develop, learn and progress, and the inspector 'must consider how well the provider and practitioners know and understand the Early Years Foundation Stage learning and development requirements' (Ofsted, 2012b: 10). Inspectors have a clear expectation that settings and schools will regularly evaluate *their own* practice to ensure that they meet all the requirements and that children are progressing well in their learning.

We have covered all the aspects of learning, development and assessment in the EYFS 2012 in this book and, in so doing, provided some tools for those already working in the early years to reflect on current practice, celebrate strengths and identify areas for further development. The 'top tips for effective practice' and 'points for reflection' throughout the book will make a useful checklist for self-evaluation, while the examples of effective practice and observations of children playing, learning and developing in their settings will have helped to illustrate the positive impact of effective support. If you are a student who is not yet involved in any setting, the examples of practice will be helpful to you.

What really makes a difference is valuing every child as a unique person, ensuring positive relationships, building an enabling environment and the quality of interaction between adults and the children. The only way we can tailor what we do to the needs of the children is through observing them in action and listening to them, talking about them with their parents and getting to know them well. Let us leave the last word to a child who has been in the nursery setting since he was 18 mths and is now just 3.

> *As Billy looked through his profile folder with his mother he talked about the photos of things which have been particularly important for him. Most often these were learning experiences in the outdoor area and were especially fun or exciting. Looking at a series of photos of him on different pieces of climbing equipment he said: 'I'm doing slides and ... through the tunnel!' Then he put his finger to his lips and pointed to another photo: 'Shh ... I'm doing ... shh! I'm hiding! We had to be quiet. Shh!'*

References

Early Years Foundation Stage 2012 Statutory Framework and government-endorsed guidance documents

Department of Health (2009) *Healthy Child Programme: Two Year Review*. Available for download from: http://www.dh.gov.uk/ prod_consum_dh/groups/dh_digitalassets/documents/digitalasset/ dh_108329.pdf.

Early Education (2012) *Development Matters in the Early Years Foundation Stage*. London: Early Education. Available for download from: www.early-education.org.uk.

National Children's Bureau (2012) *A Know How Guide, The EYFS Progress Check at Age Two*. Available for download from: www. foundationyears.org.uk.

Parents' Guide to the Early Years Foundation Stage Framework (2012) Available for download from: www.foundationyears.org.uk.

Early Years Foundation Stage (2008) London: Department for Children, Schools and Families. Available for download from: www. foundationyears.org.uk.

Allen, G. (2011) *Early Intervention: The Next Step*. London: Department for Work and Pensions. Available for download from: http://www. dwp.gov.uk/docs/early-intervention-next-steps.pdf.

Field, F. (2010) *The Foundation Years: Preventing Poor Children Becoming Poor Adults: Report of the Independent Review on Poverty and Life Chances*. London: Department for Education. Available for download from: http://webarchive.nationalarchives.gov.uk/20110120090128/ http:/povertyreview.independent.gov.uk.

Statutory Framework for the Early Years Foundation Stage: Setting the Standards for Learning, Development and Care for Children from Birth to

Five (2012) London: Department for Education. Available for download from: http://media.education.gov.uk/assets/files/pdf/eyfs%20statutory%20framework%20march%202012.pdf.

Tickell, C. (2011) *The Early Years: Foundations for Life, Health and Learning, An Independent Report on the Early Years Foundation Stage to Her Majesty's Government.* Available for download from: www.education.gov.uk/tickellreview.

Other references

Brown, B. (2008) *Equality in Action.* Stoke on Trent: Trentham Books.

Bruce, T. (2011) *Cultivating Creativity in Babies, Toddlers and Young Children* (2nd edn). London: Hodder Education.

Bruce, T., Meggitt, C. and Grenier, J. (2010) *Child Care and Education.* London: Hodder Education.

Carruthers, E. and Worthington, M. (2010) Children's mathematical development, in Bruce, T. (ed.) *Early Childhood: A Guide for Students* (2nd edn). London: Sage.

Carruthers, E. and Worthington, M. (2011) *Understanding Children's Mathematical Graphics: Beginnings in Play.* Berkshire: Open University Press/McGraw-Hill.

Cooper, L. and Doherty, J. (2010) *Physical Development.* London: Continuum International Publishing Group.

Craft, A. (2007) *Creativity and Possibility in the Early Years.* Tactyc. Available for download from: http://www.tactyc.org.uk/pdfs/Reflection-craft.pdf.

Desforges, C. and Abouchaar, A. (2003) *The Impact of Parental Involvement, Parental Support and Family Education on Pupil Achievements and Adjustment: A Literature Review.* London: Department for Education and Skills.

Dowling, M. (2005) Training materials to accompany DVD: *Extending Children's Thinking Through Their Self Chosen Activities.* London: Early Education.

Dweck, C. (2008) *Mindset: the New Psychology of Success.* New York: Random House.

Elfer, P., Goldschmied, E. and Selleck, D. (2002) *Key Persons in the Nursery: Building Relationships for Quality Provision*. London: David Fulton Publishers Ltd.

Evangelou, M., Sylva, K., Kyriacou, M., Wild, M. and Glenny, G. (2009) *Early Years Learning and Development Literature Review'*. Research Report RR176. London: Department for Children, Schools and Families. Available to download from: www.education.gov.uk/publications/RSG/publicationDetail/Page1/DCSF-RR176.

Fisher, J. (2012) Under control: the adult role in child led learning. *Nursery World*, 19 March: 19–22.

Garrick, R. (2006) *Minibeasts and More: Young Children Investigating the Natural World*. London: Early Education.

Gerhardt, S. (2004) *Why Love Matters: How Affection Shapes a Baby's Brain*. London: Routledge.

Goddard Blythe, S. (2004) *The Well Balanced Child*. Stroud: Hawthorn Press.

Goddard Blythe, S. (2011) *The Genius of Natural Childhood*. Stroud: Hawthorn Press.

Goldschmied, E. and Selleck, D. (1996) *Communication Between Babies in their First Year*. London: National Children's Bureau.

Gopnik, A., Meltzoff, A. and Kuhl, P. (1999) *How Babies Think*. London: Phoenix.

Grenier, J. (1999) All about developing positive relations with children. *Nursery World*, 16 September (reproduced in EYFS, 2007).

Hutchin, V. (2003) *Observing and Assessing for the Foundation Stage Profile*. London: Hodder & Stoughton.

Hutchin, V. (2007) *Supporting and Assessing Every Child's Learning for the Early Years Foundation Stage*. London: Hodder Education.

Hutchin, V. (2010) Meeting individual needs, in Bruce, T. (ed.) *Early Childhood: A Guide for Students*. London: Sage.

Hutchin, V. (2012) *The EYFS: A Practical Guide for Students and Professionals*. London: Hodder Education.

Kline, N. (1999) *Time to Think, Listening to Ignite the Human Mind*. London: Ward Lock/Cassell Illustrated.

Laevers, F. (2000) Forward to basics! Deep-level-learning and the experiential approach. *Early Years* 20(2).

MacNaughton, G. and Hughes, P. (2011) *Parents and Professionals in Early Childhood Settings*. Berkshire: Open University Press/McGraw-Hill.

Malloch, S. and Trevarthen, C. (eds) (2009) *Communicative Musicality. Exploring the Basis of Human Companionship*. Oxford: Oxford University Press.

National Strategies (2007) *Confident, Capable and Creative: Supporting Boys' Achievements*. London: Department for Children, Schools and Families. Available for download from: www.foundationyears.org.uk.

National Strategies (2008) *Every Child a Talker, Guidance for practitioners, 1st Instalment*. London: Department for Children, Schools and Families. Available for download from: www.foundationyears. org.uk.

National Strategies (2009a) *Children Thinking Mathematically: PSRN Essential Knowledge for Early Years Practitioners*. London: Department for Children, Schools and Families. Available for download from: www.foundationyears.org.uk.

National Strategies (2009b) *Learning, Playing and Interacting*. London: Department for Children, Schools and Families. Available for download from: www.foundationyears.org.uk.

National Strategies (2010) *Finding and Exploring Young Children's Fascinations*. London: Department for Children, Schools and Families. Available for download from: www.foundationyears. org.uk.

O'Connor, A. (2012) Prime time: physical development. *Nursery World*, 25 June–8 July 2012: 17–22.

Ofsted (2007) *The Foundation Stage: A Survey of 144 Settings*. London: Department for Education and Skills.

Ofsted (2012a) *Evaluation Schedule for Inspections of Registered Early Years Provision (July 2012)*. London: Ofsted.

Ofsted (2012b) *Conducting Early Years Inspections (September 2012)*. London: Ofsted.

Paley, V.G. (2004) *A Child's Work: The Importance of Fantasy Play*. Chicago: University of Chicago Press.

Saluja, G., Scott-Little, C. and Clifford, R.M. (2000) Readiness for school: a survey of state policies and definitions. *Early Childhood Research and Practice* 2(2), Fall.

Sheridan, M. (2008) *From Birth to Five Years: Children's Developmental Progress* (3rd edn), revised and updated by A. Sharma and H. Cockerill. London: Routledge.

Siraj-Blatchford, I., Sylva, K., Muttock, S., Gilden, R. and Bell, D. (2002) *Researching Effective Pedagogy in the Early Years (REPEY)*. Research Report 356. London: Department for Education and Skills.

Stewart, N. (2011) *How Children Learn: the Characteristics of Effective Learning*. London: Early Education.

Sylva, K., Melhuish, E.C., Sammons, P., Siraj-Blatchford, I. and Taggart, B. (2007) *Effective Pre-school and Primary Education (EPPE 3–11) (2003–2008)*. London: Institute of Education, University of London.

Vygotsky, L. (1978) *Mind in Society*. Cambridge, MA: Harvard University Press.

Wells, G. (1987) *The Meaning Makers*. London: Hodder & Stoughton.

White, J. (2008) *Playing and Learning Outdoors*. London: Routledge.

Whitehead, M. and Thompson, S. (2010) Communication, language and literacy, in Bruce, T. (ed.) *Early Childhood: A Guide for Students* (2nd edn). London: Sage.

Whitehead, M.R. (2009) *Supporting Language and Literacy Development in the Early Years* (2nd edn). Berkshire: Open University Press/McGraw-Hill.

Index

STARTING FROM THE CHILD
Teaching and Learning in the Foundation Stage
Fourth Edition

Julie Fisher

9780335246519 (Paperback)
March 2013

eBook also available

Starting from the Child supports early years practitioners to be advocates for young children and their learning needs. In the fourth edition of this highly influential and inspirational book, Julie Fisher outlines the important theories and research which should underpin best early years practice. She takes a robust and principled stand against downward pressure to formalise young children's learning too soon, and offers practical and meaningful ways to develop high quality learning and teaching in the early years.

Key features:

- How can early years practitioners build on children's competence and autonomy as effective early learners?
- How do adults get to know children sufficiently well to plan effectively for their learning needs?
- How can early years practitioners plan for high quality child-initiated experiences alongside more focused adult-initiated learning?

www.openup.co.uk   ▐▐▌ **OPEN UNIVERSITY PRESS**
                        McGraw - Hill Education

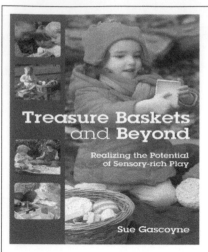

TREASURE BASKETS AND BEYOND
Realizing the Potential of Sensory-rich Play

Sue Gascoyne

9780335246441 (Paperback)
2012

eBook also available

"This accomplished book represents an impressive and important extension of previous writing in the field and is sure to expand practitioners' understanding of the fascinating medium that is the treasure basket."
Janet Moyles, Professor Emeritus, Anglia Ruskin University, UK

Watching a child play with a Treasure Basket can give a powerful insight into the wonder of children's minds; their developmental levels, interests, likes and dislikes; repeated patterns of behaviour; and even glimpses of a child's personality. This book draws extensively upon observations of children's play as well as contemporary and original research in neuroscience and sensory play, to offer fresh insights into the use and benefits of Treasure Baskets and sensory-rich play.

Key features:

- Explaining the importance of sensory play in terms of its powerful effect upon brain development and memory
- The problem solving potential of sensory rich play

www.openup.co.uk

OPEN UNIVERSITY PRESS
McGraw - Hill Education

A-Z OF PLAY IN EARLY CHILDHOOD

Janet Moyles

9780335246380 (Paperback)
2012

eBook also available

This indispensable guide uses a unique glossary format to explore some of the key themes in play in early childhood, many of which regularly arise for students, tutors, parents and practitioners. As well as covering key concepts, theories and influential figures in the field, the book considers important aspects of each construct and highlights the complexity of play in early childhood.

Key features:

- Split into a comprehensive glossary running through elements of play from A – Z, it is a useful, fun and unique companion to understanding children's play
- Original thoughts from well known early years people including Tricia David, Carol Aubrey, Angela Anning and Lilian Katz

www.openup.co.uk

OPEN UNIVERSITY PRESS
McGraw - Hill Education

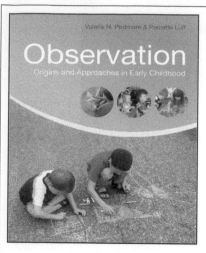

OBSERVATION
Origins and Approaches in Early Childhood

Valerie Podmore and Paulette Luff

9780335244249 (Paperback)
2012

eBook also available

"This book is an excellent resource for all those studying or working in the field of early childhood. It deals with key issues of observational processes offering a balance between theory and practical activities. It is written in a critical, engaging and informative way, with scope for interesting discussions with students, and is a useful tool for lecturers and students as in learning about observations for all involved in early childhood education."
Dr. Ioanna Palaiologou CPsychol, Lecturer, University of Hull, UK

Key features:

- An adaptation of a book that has been successful in New Zealand - updated with UK content
- Rich in examples, drawing on a variety of studies, policies and contexts to illustrate key points
- A range of practical techniques, both qualitative and quantitative for practitioners

www.openup.co.uk

OPEN UNIVERSITY PRESS
McGraw - Hill Education